DICKENS
Public Life and Private Passion

DICKENS
Public Life and Private Passion

BBC

This book is published to accompany the television series entitled *Dickens: Public Life and Private Passion*, which was first broadcast on BBC Television in 2002. Executive Producer: Andrea Miller. Produced and directed by Mary Downes and Chris Granlund. Assistant Producer: Robin Dashwood. Researcher: Jane Mayes. Production Manager: Joanna Hatley. Production Co-ordinators: Margaret Hulse and Ben Lawrie

Published by BBC Worldwide Ltd, Woodlands, 80 Wood Lane, London W12 0TT

First published 2002
Copyright © Peter Ackroyd 2002
The moral right of the author has been asserted.

ISBN 0 563 53473 7

Commisioning Editor: Emma Shackleton
Project Editor: Helena Caldon. Copy-editor: Esther Jagger. Art Director: Linda Blakemore.
Designer: Paul Vater at Sugar Free. Picture Researcher: Sarah Hopper.

Set in Spectrum
Printed and bound in Italy by LEGO Spa
Colour separations by Kestrel Digital Colour, Chelmsford

DICKENS
Public Life and Private Passion

CONTENTS

CHAPTER ONE

The trials of childhood

Charles Dickens was from the beginning as much a child of his time as of his natural parents, John and Elizabeth Dickens. His childhood was spent in sight of the sea, at the beginning of the nineteenth century, when Britain's imperial destiny was already being formed upon the waves. He was born in Portsea, just outside Portsmouth, on 7 February 1812, only seven years after Nelson defeated Napoleon at the Battle of Trafalgar. It is significant, therefore, that his father was employed by the Navy Pay Office and, for the next ten years, he moved with his family to a succession of naval ports. In his later fiction he is always fond of sailors and of midshipmen, like Captain Cuttle, no doubt because they reminded him of the happiest years of his early life.

Charles was the second of six surviving children, and was from infancy marked out as singular and precocious. He had no doubt inherited some of his gifts. His father was a talkative and cheerful man whose benign disposition did not prevent him from wishing to be known as a 'gentleman'; his mother was a vivacious woman with a sharp eye and a keen sense of humour. He admitted later that he had been born an actor, and as a child became an astute singer of comic songs with all the actions and all the attitudes. In his later public readings he was hailed as the greatest performer of his age, but his genius was first nourished in the local taverns where his father brought him to sing and dance.

Top: Dickens's birthplace in Portsea.
Middle and bottom: His parents; Elizabeth Dickens and John Dickens.
Opposite: Charles Dickens as a young author.

His parents also took him to the small theatres of the neighbourhood, and Dickens maintained his affection for actors and acting until the last days of his life. As a child he owned a toy theatre, and from that time forward he never lost his vision of the world as a stage. It could be argued that all of his novels sprang out of that vision; certainly his own life was, as it were, encircled by stage fire.

He was also a very nervous and sensitive boy, immensely susceptible to slights and disappointments of every kind, but at the same time wide-eyed and alert to all the details of his childhood world. In much later life he could recall the texture of the picture books he read, and the mechanics of all the toys he played with; he could recall the smell of the adults' clothes, and could exactly reproduce the habits and features of his neighbours. He went to school, too, and began his reading of those eighteenth-century novels — *Tom Jones*, *Roderick Random*, *Peregrine Pickle* — which affected his own fiction.

But these happy and agreeable times did not endure. If they had lasted, it is possible to argue that Dickens would never have become the greatest novelist of his century. Misfortune, hardship and terror made him what he was. John Dickens was posted to the Admiralty in London, and of course his family were obliged to move with him into the capital which even then was acquiring its reputation as the 'Great Wen', the 'Oven' and 'Babylon'.

At the age of ten the young Charles Dickens arrived in Camden Town, then a straggling suburb surrounded by fields. He found it dreary and unsettling. He had been removed from the friends of his own age but, more importantly, his family gave no thought to his education. There is no doubt that he was a bright and ambitious boy, with dreams of becoming a famous and successful man. Now he was reduced to cleaning his father's boots and running errands for the rest of his family. He never forgot this fall from hopefulness and security; indeed, his adult personality was in part formed from it.

The family fortunes were being steadily reduced. His father, it seems, was borrowing money that he could not repay, and it is an open question as to whether he was drinking or gambling it away. The young boy played with his

Left: The house in Bayham Street, London.

toy theatre and walked down dreary Bayham Street to look at the dome of
St Paul's Cathedral rising above the mist and smoke of monstrous London.
How were the family to survive? Mrs Dickens started a school, but nobody
came. It was time, then, for the young Dickens to earn his keep. A friend of
the family was managing a blacking warehouse by the Thames, and at the age
of twelve, for a salary of six shillings a week, Charles Dickens was put to work
there. His job was to seal the boot blacking in pots and paste on labels; it was
dirty and smelly work, shared with two or three other poor boys. He believed
that he would never be clean again.

*No words can express the secret agony of my soul as I sunk into this companion-
ship; compared these everyday associates with those of my happier childhood;
and felt my early hopes of growing up to be a learned and distinguished
man crushed in my breast. The deep remembrance of the sense I had of being
utterly neglected and hopeless; of the shame I felt in my misery, cannot be
written. My whole nature was so penetrated with grief and humiliation of such
considerations that even now, famous and caressed and happy, I often forget in
my dreams that I have a dear wife and children; even that I am a man; and
wander desolately back to that time of my life.*

Above: Marshalsea prison, Southwark where John Dickens was incarcerated.

But then a further nightmare descended upon him. Eleven days after Charles first entered the blacking factory, his father was arrested for debt and consigned to the Marshalsea prison in the neighbourhood of Southwark. Mrs Dickens and the youngest members of the family moved into his prison cell, while Charles found lodgings nearby. The factory and the prison, then, represented Dickens's first true encounter with London. It could be said that these were also the two most important institutions of nineteenth-century civilization, and so from an early age he intuitively understood the nature of that civilization. He became its most effective spokesman and its most bitter opponent. He was a genius precisely because he stood in symbolic relationship with his own time.

My father was waiting for me in the prison lodge and we went up to his room
(on the top storey but one), and cried very much. And he told me, I remember,
to take warning by the Marshalsea, and to observe that if a man had twenty
pounds a year, and spent nineteen shillings and sixpence, he would be happy;
but that a shilling spent the other way would make him wretched.

In those early years, however, he feared that he might turn into a little vagabond or thief. That is how he was able to create Fagin and the Artful Dodger with such a powerful and passionate persuasion; they were particles of himself, images of Charles Dickens as he might have been and, somewhere deep down within him, still was. Fagin was the name of one of his little labouring companions. The name stayed in his mind as an emblem of horror, even though the real Bob Fagin was kindly and sympathetic. One day, in the depths of his mental agonies, Charles Dickens fell upon the floor of the blacking factory in a fit which lasted all afternoon; it was the harbinger of a pain in his left side which would

Above: The blacking factory by the Thames where Dickens was sent to work.

recur at periods of anxiety throughout his life. Bob Fagin was the one who nursed him through it. He was repaid by giving his name to a ferocious villain.

But then, as in Dickens's novels, the horror and the nightmare lifted to provide a fairy-tale ending. When critics say that his fiction is not 'true to life', the response can only be that it was true to *his* life. His father came into a legacy, from his grandmother, and the Dickens family were at last set free. But it was not quite the same happy family. Elizabeth Dickens insisted that Charles should still earn his living in the blacking factory, and so the boy was sent back to the filthy warehouse by the river. He never forgave her for what seemed to him to be an act of treachery, and his mother was later savagely satirized in his novels as Mrs Nickleby and others. They were never close again.

John Dickens, however, proved his salvation; in a momentary fit of gentlemanly pride, no longer able to endure the sight of his eldest son as a poor labouring boy, he removed him from his lamentable employment. So although home was still precious, it was not secure. It might be snatched away. Life was a perilous business. It had to be mastered. It had to be organized and controlled. It had to be given a formal shape; an artistic shape. His childhood experiences had created the man and the artist equally.

From that hour until this, my father and mother have been stricken dumb upon it. I have never heard the least allusion to it, however far off and remote, from either of them. I have never in any burst of confidence with anyone, my own wife not excepted, raised the curtain I then dropped, thank God.

He could now fulfil his earliest ambition of becoming an educated man, and was enrolled once more at a school. He stayed at the Wellington Academy for only two years, but those years formed a natural barrier between his unhappy past and the successful future that he wished to carve for himself. He was no longer the filthy labourer but the model of the healthy schoolboy, very neat and very clean. He seemed to be, or acted the

Above: Dickens in the blacking factory.

part of, the son of a gentleman. According to his fellow pupils, he was prone to laughing immoderately at nothing in particular. Well might he laugh. He had escaped.

Of course, he lied about his past. He never would stop lying or, shall we say, elaborating upon the truth. It was part of his genius. He said that his old existence 'became so strange to me that I hardly believed in it'. After leaving his school friends he was enrolled as a lawyer's clerk in the firm of Ellis and Blackmore, where he made the acquaintance of all those young clerks who would eventually appear in his fiction in the semblance of Mr Guppy, Uriah Heep and a score of others.

Among these contemporaries he soon gained a reputation as a mimic, mainly of 'low' London types – the types with whom he had lived and worked as a child. How better to exorcize the past than to laugh at it? He also knew London intimately. He knew that the coachmakers worked in Long Acre and

the clockmakers in Clerkenwell, that the dentists were in Finsbury Pavement and the hatmakers in Bermondsey. He knew the peculiar odour of each area. He even knew the different types of pet in areas as diverse as Harley Street and the Seven Dials.

In particular, he knew the little theatres that clustered around Catherine Street and Holywell Street off the Strand. He wanted to be a comic actor and, for a small sum paid to the manager, he could perform on these stages in front of a vociferous and often obscene London audience. Ever since childhood he had been a performer and a speaker, always seeming more himself for taking on another part. It is as if he were a company of actors within one suit. He even requested an audition with the stage manager of Covent Garden, but a fortunate illness forced him to cancel his appointment – fortunate, at least, for the books that were then no more than shadows in his head. He was not yet seventeen years old, but it seems as if his genius was already forming his destiny.

*Above: The young Dickens.
Below: Covent Garden
marketplace.*

CHAPTER TWO

The people must be amused

His mature character was also being formed out of passion and strife. He met a banker's daughter, a year older than himself; her name was Maria Beadnell and immediately he became obsessed with her. It is one of the secrets of his character that he flung himself furiously into situations without properly judging the consequences; delay and indecision were anathema to him. Yet it seems that Maria Beadnell did not return his affection in quite such

a glowing manner, and in a letter he told her that their brief meetings 'never failed to prove a fertile source of wretchedness and misery'. Her parents had discovered, too, that John Dickens had once been detained in a debtors' prison, which, as far as they were concerned, deepened the unsuitability of the match. All the while Charles would stand outside Maria Beadnell's bedroom window, at two or three in the morning, and in voluminous letters pour out his misery. 'I have been so long used to inward wretchedness and real, real misery that it matters little, very little to me what others may think or what becomes of me.' And then again, 'I have borne more from you than I do believe any living creature breathing ever bore from a woman before.'

Left: Maria Beadnell (in later years).
Opposite: Charles Dickens aged twenty-seven.

There are some insights here into Dickens's emotional life. He truly believed that no one had ever suffered as much, and this is of a piece with his later protestations or over-statements. Everything to do with him he deemed to be unique. He retreated easily into terrible wretchedness, as if his high spirits and general gaiety were no more than a carapace to conceal some internal core of suffering that nothing could assuage. His fervour, and his misery, were therefore pitched very high indeed. When he told Maria Beadnell that 'I have never loved and I can never love any human creature breathing but yourself', he was once more prone to the over-exaggeration that comes very close to melodrama.

Yet it ought to be noted how fine and skilful a writer the young Dickens had already become, with a natural gift for impassioned utterance that may derive in part from his experience upon the stage. It is hard to distinguish between what he is feeling and what he is enacting, and in that ambiguous area his mature character was formed. It becomes clear that he was already over-sensitive to slights, and that he was all too ready to fall into the depths of self-pity at a moment's notice; it is true, too, that a fear of humiliation also became one of the constant forces in his life.

Above: Riverine scene in London.

He never forgot Maria Beadnell, and declared at a later date that his thwarted passion 'made so deep an impression on me that I refer to it a habit of suppression which now belongs to me, which I know is no part of my original nature, but which makes me chary of showing my affections, even to my children, except when they are very young'. He did not wish to be hurt again; he did not wish his openly expressed feelings to be met with reserve or disapproval. Just as his childhood trials had nerved him to face the world with will and ambition, so emotional hurt taught him reticence and repression. In his adult years, for example, he never told his family about the episode in the blacking factory. It was still too close to him. That is also why he lavished such affection upon his characters, and why the depths of his passionate nature were poured into his fiction. If they did emerge in his life, they were terrible to behold.

He had hoped, in these earlier years, that a career upon the stage would lift him out of the poor world of the lawyer's clerk. Having been thwarted in this ambition, however, he quickly settled upon the next best option. He would become a shorthand reporter in the newly emerging political press, and then hope to earn fifteen guineas a week rather than a clerk's salary of some fifteen shillings. And so he set to work with his usual ferocious energy and excitement. The shorthand course usually took three years to master; Dickens managed it within three months.

Whatever I have tried to do in life, I have tried with all my heart to do well; whatever I have devoted myself to, I have devoted myself to completely; in great aims and in small, I have always been thoroughly in earnest.

At the age of nineteen he joined the *Mirror of Parliament*, and was at once plunged into the tumultuous and chaotic politics of his time. It was a period in which the ablest administrators were intent upon taking the eighteenth century out of nineteenth-century England, particularly in the matter of

Above: Charles Dickens as a young reporter.

electoral reform. Dickens began reporting parliamentary debates just at the time when the Reform Bill was being enacted into law, accompanied by riots and demonstrations throughout the country in its favour. There was a new Factory Act, controlling the number of hours that children might work, and a new Poor Law was being introduced as an efficient way of dealing with the poor and the infirm.

He knew all about working children, of course, and the threat of poverty had never been lifted during his own childhood. So he threw himself into parliamentary reporting with all the haste and sharpness of his passionate

and impulsive nature. He flew along, in wagons and post-chaises and coaches, to catch all the latest news. The mud used to pour in through the windows as he sat with his papers on his knees trying to re-create the speeches he had heard.

And then, to earn a little more than his parliamentary salary, he began to try his hand at sketches and stories. In a sense he had been preparing for them all his life. His first tales concern feckless families, improvident persons in search of an inheritance, the lower middle class teetering on the twin edges of respectability or poverty. He knew these characters; he had lived with them and worked with them. More importantly, he had shared their fears and their desires. Here are boarders and lodging-house keepers, young ladies pursued sentimentally by young clerks, solemn bachelors and precocious children, all of them conceived in the light of that 'immoderate laughter' which the young Dickens had exhibited as a schoolboy. Some of the themes and subjects were even closer to home; one story is set in a 'lock-up' or 'sponging-house', the preliminary step towards the debtors' prison, where only a short time earlier Charles Dickens's father had once again been confined.

Above: The Grapes at Limehouse, London.

The room — which was a small, confined den — was partitioned off into boxes like the common-room of some inferior eating-house. The dirty floor had evidently been as long a stranger to the scrubbing-brush as to carpet or floor-cloth: and the ceiling was completely blackened by the flare of the oil-lamp by which the room was lighted at night. The grey ashes on the edges of the tables, and the cigar ends which were plentifully scattered about the dusty grate, fully accounted for the intolerable smell of tobacco which pervaded the place.

'A Passage in the Life of Mr Watkins Tottle' from Sketches by Boz

The young Dickens was turning the most fearful and unpleasant scenes into laughter. It is worth remembering that his first ambition was to become a comic actor and, in these early stories, he was clearly turning the ordinary world of anxiety or strife into theatre and pantomime. That was his way of understanding, and indeed of controlling, reality. In that sense his art never really changed, even if it was immeasurably deepened and enlarged. It is significant, for example, that there are characters in these early stories who anticipate his later fictional creations. A miser named Nicodemus Dumps is an uncanny early version of Ebenezer Scrooge, and a family named the Kitterbells are astoundingly similar to the Cratchits.

Dickens invented the pseudonym of 'Boz' as the appropriate author of these sketches, and their popularity was such that they very soon eclipsed his reputation as a parliamentary reporter. As a result he was asked to provide stories and essays for other newspapers. These descriptive pieces, largely concerning London, provide the best possible entry into the life of the early

Above: The slums of the Seven Dials area in London.

nineteenth-century city with its cab-drivers and its pawnbrokers, its gin shops and its fairs, its pleasure gardens and its private theatres. As a young clerk he had been known for his intimate knowledge of urban life, and in these sketches that close acquaintance is found *in excelsis*. He noticed everything, from the exact colour of the sign above a second-hand clothing shop to the way London cab-drivers greeted one another with 'the solemn lifting of the little finger of the right hand'. Throughout his life he possessed a truly phenomenal memory. If he walked down a street, he could effortlessly recall the name and disposition of the shops that he had passed; he could remember the names and occupations of people many years after a brief meeting with them.

All these qualities are to be observed in the sketches, to which are added a formal fluency and an inventive power that turn local journalism into universal art. One publisher, John Macrone, was so impressed that he asked Dickens if he might publish a volume of these short works, to be accompanied by the illustrations of the illustrious George Cruikshank. Dickens readily agreed, and on 7 February 1836, *Sketches by Boz* was published to almost universal acclaim. It was its author's twenty-fourth birthday, but he had given a present to the world.

Three days after its publication the young – the very young – Dickens received another offer. The firm of Chapman and Hall had decided to print a monthly series on the adventures of some Cockney sportsmen, whose dissipations in the countryside might provide moments of facetiousness in an early nineteenth-century manner; they already possessed an illustrator, Edward Seymour, but they needed an author to provide the text. They had approached several journalists, but to no immediate effect. But now a rapid perusal of *Sketches by Boz* suggested the ideal writer for the work; 'Boz' was comic and observant at the same time, and his happily fluent manner was perfectly suited to the demands of a monthly fiction.

Top: George Cruikshank.
Above: Title page of Sketches by Boz.

William Hall visited Dickens in his bachelor lodgings in Furnival's Inn, and he had no sooner opened the door to him than Dickens uttered a cry of recognition. This was the man who had sold him a copy of the *Monthly Magazine* in which Dickens's first story had appeared; there could have been no better omen. Hall then put to him the following proposition – twenty thousand words per month, at a rate of fourteen guineas, the series to be completed after twenty monthly instalments. Dickens considered the proposal and, as he informed a friend, 'the work will be no joke, but the emolument is too tempting to resist'. Throughout his life Dickens would be preoccupied with the making of money; he was liberal and generous to others, but the early experience of poverty had helped to form his character. He constantly seemed to believe that he was on the verge of bankruptcy, and worried incessantly about his income. He would always take on work, and yet more work, in order to feel secure. In *A Christmas Carol* Scrooge is told, of his miserliness, that 'You fear the world too much.' There was more than a touch of Scrooge in Dickens himself.

So he willingly accepted William Hall's proposal and yet, in what would become an entirely characteristic way, turned it upon its head in order to make it more agreeable to himself. In all of his subsequent dealings with publishers, in fact, he would retain an almost wilful independence in the expediting and rewriting of contracts. He soon became well enough aware both of his genius and of his popularity always to triumph over less shrewd businessmen.

So the young author informed Hall that he could not write about Cockney sportsmen, having only a very limited acquaintance with sport

Above: Manuscript of A Christmas Carol.

himself, but would instead write upon whatever subject he pleased. He already knew a wide range of London 'types', as his sketches had proved so decisively, and only needed a narrative to set them in motion. Hall, no doubt impressed by Dickens's charm as well as his audacity, concurred.

And then, in Dickens's simple phrase, 'I thought of Mr Pickwick.' Or rather he recalled a coach proprietor from Bath whose name was emblazoned on his vehicles; the name was Moses Pickwick. But he did not only think of Pickwick; he thought of Mr Jingle, he thought of Mr Wardle, he thought of Sam Weller. That personage's entry in the fourth number of *The Pickwick Papers* guaranteed the novel's fortune. He made the world laugh. Sam Weller was a true original. He was the first Cockney hero, the first to use the sharp Cockney humour that Dickens knew from the streets. Dickens had put down on paper a type that everyone recognized, but had never before seen in print.

'Person's a waitin',' said Sam, epigrammatically.

'Does the person want me, Sam?' inquired Mr Pickwick.

'He wants you particklar; and no one else'll do, as the Devil's private secretary

said ven he fetched away Doctor Faustus.'

'He. Is it a gentleman?'

'A wery good imitation o' one, if it an't.'

The Pickwick Papers, *Chapter XV*

That was his genius. He was creating a world in which everyone felt at home, yet a thousand times brighter than the real thing. He was creating reality for the new reading public. Pickwick was triumphant. It began with a circulation of four hundred copies and ended with one of forty thousand. It was talked about more than national politics. It was more *real* than national politics. There were Pickwick cigars, Pickwick coats and Pickwick hats. 'Pickwick' was inscribed upon one of the great pyramids of Egypt. And he will last as long.

Above: Mr Pickwick.

But Dickens was only just beginning, and almost immediately on starting work upon *Pickwick* he engaged himself in half a dozen other schemes, a single one of which would have been enough for any ordinary man. This was always to be an aspect of his character, this need to deluge himself in work as if there were a fire within him that could not be extinguished. He loved to wear himself down, and his only refuge was in action. It sprang partly out of his desire for money, but partly also out of the satisfaction of getting work done. He was the consummate professional writer who kept to his deadlines over a lifetime.

Three months after the first number of *The Pickwick Papers*, he signed a contract to produce another novel entitled *Gabriel Vardon, the Locksmith of London*; this eventually emerged into the light as *Barnaby Rudge*. He also wrote a pamphlet entitled *Sunday Under Three Heads*, in which he excoriated those public figures who wished to ban Sunday recreation for the working classes. As he was to say in a later novel, the people must be amused. He had agreed to write a second series of *Sketches by Boz*, and in that capacity he undertook various expeditions to the more colourful or notorious areas of London. He also found time to write a play entitled *The Village Coquettes*, performed together with another play of his composition, *The Strange Gentleman*.

Dickens's dramas have not enjoyed the same reputation or reception as his fiction, and indeed they are somewhat laboured affairs. This may seem surprising in so theatrical a novelist, whose first thoughts were of the stage, but early nineteenth-century drama demanded a certain naturalism or realism. Dickens's novels are fantastic and wayward, with the dialogue pitched to an exquisite key of unreality; the speech of his dramatic characters is

Top: Pickwick's Coaching House.
Above: Sam Weller.

amusing but somehow flattened by the conventions of the period. His relative failure as a dramatist might, however, give pause to those who consider that in the present century Dickens would have been a natural and appropriate writer of television drama; it does not seem likely.

Even while engaged in these multifarious literary activities the young Dickens was still employed as a journalist, reporting on election campaigns, public dinners and sensational trials. Such was his confidence in his own ability and in his energetic perseverance, however, that he agreed to supply eight additional pages of story to each month's instalment of *The Pickwick Papers*. The text was now the most important consideration, even though in the course of early publication he found a young man, Hablot Knight Browne, who under the pseudonym of 'Phiz' would remain his illustrator for many years.

He had found another companion, too, of a more intimate sort. In the spring of 1836, after a year's engagement, he married the daughter of one of his newspaper colleagues. Catherine Hogarth had been nineteen when they had first met, just four years younger than Dickens, and it seems that their attraction was mutual and obvious. She was a placid, almost quiescent, beauty whose blue eyes and dark hair had already become for Dickens an exquisite 'type'. She was not quick or energetic, although it might be surmised that her lover had energy and quickness for a thousand households; she was, if anything, slow and gentle. Although in later years that slowness would be a source of irritation or embarrassment to Dickens, at the time it must have seemed a distinct advantage in the partner of so quixotic and restless a man. Her soft and endearing disposition was for him a refuge and a source of comfort in what rapidly became – to use one of his favourite phrases – the battle of life.

Above: Catherine Hogarth.

It ought to be recalled here that his previous love affair had been marked by savage anxiety and distress, when the 'first love' of the romantic imagination had turned sour. Maria Beadnell had been petty and coquettish, and her rejection of his passion was for him a stern warning that he should not and could not betray his own inner feelings. He remained defensive for the rest of his life, as he admitted, and even in his youthful relationship to Catherine there is an air of masterliness and self-control that might have acted as an oblique warning concerning his future conduct. In only his second letter to her he chastised her gently for certain deficiencies in her temperament, in a manner which would become entirely characteristic of him.

> *If a hasty temper produce this strange behaviour, acknowledge it when I give you the opportunity — not once or twice, but again and again. If a feeling of you know what — a capricious restlessness of you can't tell what, and a desire to teaze, you don't know why, give rise to it — overcome it; it will never make you more amiable, I more fond, or either of us, more happy. If three weeks or three months of my society has wearied you, do not trifle with me, using me as any other toy that suits your humour for the moment; but make the acknowledgment to me frankly — I shall not forget you lightly, but you will need no second warning.*
>
> *Charles Dickens to Catherine Hogarth, late May 1835*

It is clear that he was still immensely sensitive to slights or hurts of any kind, and was inclined to withdraw into self-pity; his language is couched in tones of fond concern, but it is not difficult to discern a note of defensiveness in his reproaches. His mother had, in his opinion, betrayed him by dispatching him to the blacking factory. Maria Beadnell had rejected his advances in what he believed to be a thoroughly heartless manner. He was determined never to be hurt by a woman again. He would have to remain in control.

What Catherine Hogarth discerned of the young Dickens is an open question. Here was a handsome and ambitious young man, whose writings were already being applauded by her father and others; he was funny, spirited and energetic. Her father no doubt recommended the suit. So you might say that she acquiesced in the match. Neither party could have foreseen, however, the strange pilgrimage that they would take together.

They were married at St Luke's church in Chelsea, and set off for a week's honeymoon in Chalk, a village in the area of Kent where Dickens had spent some of his earliest years. There was always some force that propelled him back to the first scenes of his life, as if he might draw some sustenance and comfort from them. They reminded him of how much he had achieved already, perhaps, in the altered circumstances of his life. The honeymoon lasted only a week, however, since he had to return to London in order to continue work on his various projects. Work was always the keystone of his life, and nothing in the world could take him from it. His new wife must already have realized this cardinal fact, and noticed also how restless and impatient he became when away from his desk; it was to be the condition of their marriage. Dickens was always climbing the mountains of his ambitions

Top left: A letter about Pickwick to the publisher, Richard Bentley.
Above: Furnival's Inn.

and his desires, but he seldom spared any thought for those who were forced
to travel with him.

He and Catherine settled for a while in his lodgings in Furnival's Inn, one
of the Inns of Court in London, but the growing success of *Pickwick* and of his
other writings allowed them to move into a house in Doughty Street.
Catherine's younger sister, Mary, joined them as companion. She was now
fifteen, and Dickens had already conceived the strangest and most innocent
passion for her. He was always drawn to virginal young women, as if he might
then reproduce the infant relationship between himself and his sister which
had rendered happy his earliest years.

'PICKWICK TRIUMPHANT' he wrote in
the full flood of his exuberance. But already he
was looking beyond his immediate success and
had begun to speculate upon 'my fame', as if
the whole avenue of his future life had been
laid open for his inspection. 'If I were to live a
hundred years,' he wrote to his publishers,
'and write three novels in each, I should never
be so proud of any of them as I am of Pickwick.'
He also expressed the hope that after his death
'Pickwick will be found on many a dusty shelf.' Certainly he was now self-
assured to the point of bravado. He broke a theatrical rule by presenting himself
before the audience of one of his plays for a series of 'curtain calls'. But his high
opinion of himself was at the same time shared by others. Elizabeth Barrett,
later to become the wife of Robert Browning, believed that the young Dickens
was 'to be the next great benefactor of the age to Sir Walter Scott'. It was a
remarkable tribute, since Scott had dominated the life and the literature of the
previous generation to an unprecedented extent.

It had all seemed to happen by chance, or accident, except that in the career
of genius there is no such thing as chance. *The Pickwick Papers* had begun as an

Top: Mary Hogarth.
Above: Craddock's Cottage, where Charles and Catherine spent their honeymoon.

extension of Dickens's journalism, with the same playful inconsequence and rapid observation. But, as he continued its composition, he discovered the resources of his own invention; he literally found himself as he developed the story of the Pickwickians. The narrative takes imaginative fire as it goes along, and is immeasurably strengthened and deepened by Dickens's steadily enlarging vision. It has often been noted, for example, how serious and even tragic scenes are introduced within the context of overwhelmingly comic action; the episodes concerning Mr Pickwick's incarceration in the Fleet prison for non-

payment of a fine are testimony to the young novelist's range of expression. They must bear some relation to his own immediate past, when his father had been confined within the Marshalsea, but they also play a role in the larger pattern of the novel.

Indeed, this conflation of comic and tragic, pathetic and pantomimic, would become characteristic of his art. He called the effect one of 'streaky, well-cured bacon' and he used the same techniques until the end of his writing career. But in some sense the contrasts and varia-tions reflect his own character as much as his fictional predilections. Everyone noticed how odd and contrary he was. He could be all merriment and laughter at one point and then, at the next, his eyes were said to flash 'like danger lamps'. He could be familiar and cordial with strangers, but wilful and stubborn with his friends; he could talk freely and easily to the unhappy and the outcast, but was noticeably reticent with his wife and his own children. In the same way he celebrated food and drink in his fiction but, in his life, he ate little and drank less. Yet out of these contradictions, or disturbances, he fashioned his art.

The success of *Pickwick* meant that he could eventually relinquish his post as a reporter, but not without a valedictory message to his editor to the

Above: A scene from Oliver Twist *— Oliver dares to ask for more.*

effect that 'I have again and again… done
what was always before considered impossible,
and what in all probability will never be
accomplished again'. Dickens never under-
estimated his own powers. Yet even though
he had abandoned reporting, he did not
wholly leave journalism. He agreed to take on
the editorship of a new monthly magazine,
Bentley's Miscellany, which offered a wholly
characteristic mixture of fiction, articles
and reviews; the editorial role was one that

appealed to Dickens, who seems to have seen it as a more literary form of theatrical management. In fact he remained an editor, for a variety of periodicals,
until the end of his life.

It could even be suggested that he was as much a journalist as novelist,
in the sense that he took up the events of the day and used them as the
material for his art. This is nowhere more evident than in the novel that he
began to write as a serial for his new magazine. It began life under the title
'The Public Life of Mr Tulrumble', but on its second appearance it had been
renamed *Oliver Twist*. In this tale of a parish boy's progress Dickens refashioned
his own childhood neglect into a fantasy of distress and suffering, yet at the
same time he proceeded with a concerted attack upon the New Poor Law,
the provisions of which were only then being enforced. Part of his genius lay
in his ability to mingle private fantasies with public issues, so it is difficult to
disentangle the two; that is why his self-communings have all the force of
polemical statement while his social polemic has the intensity of inner
conviction. It is a potent combination.

It was only to be expected that this young and successful novelist should
also now be something of a social 'catch'. He was invited to join the Garrick
Club, and for the first time in his career he began to attract the company of

Top: London housing underneath the new railway.
Above: A front page of Bentley's Miscellany.

other writers. His first entry into literary society seems to have been a modest one. 'I kept very quiet, purposely,' he wrote to the publisher of his new magazine. 'Since I have been a successful author, I have seen how much ill-will and jealousy there is afloat, and I have acquired an excellent character as a quiet, modest fellow. I like to assume a virtue, though I have it not...' It should never be forgotten that Dickens was always a consummate actor in the company of other people, and this assumption of reticence is wholly characteristic.

In many respects, however, he had a passion for friendship. Throughout his life he turned his friends into an extended family, with all the privileges and disadvantages of that intimate connection. He was always a convivial and benevolent man, much given to facetious humour and uncannily accurate impersonations, whose withdrawn and sensitive nature found its happiest expression in laughter. There was one friend in particular he made at this time. John Forster was a young man, originally from Newcastle-on-Tyne, who had already made his name as a journalist and reviewer; he was slightly younger than Dickens, but their friendship was immediate and indeed permanent. It was Forster to whom Dickens turned in all the crises of his life, both financial and domestic, and it would be Forster who wrote the first major biography of the novelist. Forster could be pompous, stentorian and over-bearing, but his true qualities of faithfulness and eager benevolence were those that Dickens saw and embraced. He never had a truer friend.

It is Forster, too, who provides the most delightful description of Dickens in the first heat of his success. 'He had a capital forehead, a firm nose with full wide nostrils, eyes wonderfully beaming with intellect and running over with humour and cheerfulness, and a rather prominent mouth strongly marked with sensibility.' This is the portrait of the artist as a young man, an artist who knows, moreover, that he has all the world before him. But Forster noticed in

Above: John Forster.

his formidable face other qualities 'which no time could change, and which remained implanted on it unalterably to the last'. He observed in particular 'the quickness, keenness, and practical power, the eager, restless, energetic outlook on each several feature, that seemed to tell so little of the student or writer of books, and so much of the man of action and business in the world. Light and motion flashed from every part of it.'

Forster's emphasis upon his keen practicality and application to the business of the world had already been substantiated in the young novelist's dealings with publishers, but it also reflects upon Dickens's practical involvement in all the affairs of the day. There never was a writer less inclined to lock himself up in an ivory tower, or to profess the doctrine of 'art for art's sake'; he wanted to be read by as many people as possible and, to that end, carefully arranged his fictions to appeal as much to the reading clubs of working-class men as to the solitary study of the bishop or doctor.

But it was his genius to combine widespread popularity with a genuine if wild streak of poetry, to convince the reader of fanciful or fabulous things while making them laugh and cry, to conflate realism and symbolism in words that represent the first true urban myth of the nineteenth century. That is why he was able to begin *Oliver Twist* at the same time as he was continuing work on *The Pickwick Papers*; they were part of the same vision. It has often been remarked that the terrible pathos of Oliver is set strangely beside the jocular and almost saintly benevolence of Pickwick, but in truth they spring from the same impassioned source of feeling and observation. Laughter and misery went hand in hand through the streets of London, where the poorest lay huddled and dying in doorways a few yards from the mansions of the rich; this sensibility, this condition of the world, is one that runs deeply through all of Charles Dickens's novels.

Above: Oliver Twist.

CHAPTER THREE
Writing and reform

In his new family home in Doughty Street, Dickens would work each morning on both *Pickwick* and *Oliver*. His wife, Catherine, had given birth to their first child – a son promptly christened Charles – but immediately succumbed to what must have been a form of post-natal depression. She was to bear ten more children, as well as to suffer several miscarriages, and so this depression did not bode well for her; in the annals of literary history very little is said about the suffering and generally silent partner, but the plaintive life of Catherine Dickens deserves some mention here.

There was further misery to descend upon what seemed a happy and prospering household. On returning from the theatre with Charles and Catherine Dickens, Mary Hogarth went upstairs to her bed in 'her usual delightful spirits', according to Dickens, when suddenly she uttered a cry; she had collapsed and Dickens, after calling for a doctor, placed her body upon the narrow bed. She lingered there throughout that night and the following morning before succumbing to the effects of heart disease. 'Thank God she died in my arms,' Dickens wrote to an old friend, 'and the very last words she whispered were of me…' This may seem, in retrospect, a little egotistical, but in the extremity of his grief the social niceties were not observed. His pain was

Top: Dickens with Catherine and her sister, Mary Hogarth.
Above: Charles Dickens Junior.
Opposite: Lord Birkenhead opens the Dickens Museum at his former home, 48 Doughty Street, London WC1.

too great to be stifled. 'You cannot conceive,' he wrote, 'the misery in which this dreadful event has plunged us.' He arranged for 'YOUNG, BEAUTIFUL, AND GOOD' to be engraved on her tombstone.

Then he did an extraordinary thing. He took Mary's clothes and placed them in a box or cupboard; for several years he would take them out and look at them. He took a ring from her finger and put it on his own, keeping it there until his death. He determined that he would eventually be buried in Mary's grave, as if he might then be identified with all that was 'beautiful' and 'good'. It would not be going too far to say that he came to idolize the memory of

Mary Hogarth. She was constantly present in his thoughts; he even dreamed of her. More importantly, her image emerges in all the portraits of doomed or suffering young women that enter his fiction – Dora, Little Nell and Florence Dombey among them.

After the funeral he recuperated at a small farm in Hampstead and, for the first and last time in his life, he did not meet his deadline. No number of *The Pickwick Papers* emerged in that month, and the hiatus sparked the usual rumours about his general mental or physical health. One of the disadvantages of genius is the malice or incomprehension that it arouses in others. One of its virtues, however, is its resources of energy and renewal. So, after a period of intense mourning, he set back briskly to work. The conclusion of *The Pickwick Papers* was heralded with a great banquet in which all of Dickens's new friends and associates joined; perhaps more significantly, as far as Dickens was concerned, his publishers presented him with a cheque for £2500 as a token of their gratitude. *Oliver Twist* was also being pursued with his usual éclat, and such was the novelist's new-found popularity that several dramatic versions of both novels were to be seen in the metropolis.

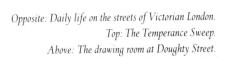

Opposite: Daily life on the streets of Victorian London.
Top: The Temperance Sweep.
Above: The drawing room at Doughty Street.

His private life also seemed to be a succession of parties, junketings and expeditions. He had already acquired the habit of walking great distances, alone or in company, and it was not unusual for him to cover fifteen or twenty miles in a pedestrian session that wearied everyone but him. It was one of his fixed opinions that, in the life of a professional writer, the hours of exercise should match those of composition; it was, he said, the best means of blowing off superfluous steam.

In fact the image of Dickens walking through the streets of the city is a central one for any understanding of the workings of his imagination. He said always that he needed the 'magic lantern' of London's streets to keep his vision bright, and his immersion in the anonymous crowds of the city materially affected the nature of his invention. He needed their energy and their motion, their anonymity and their cohesion. It was as if a thousand different stories swirled around him. He was known everywhere, from East Smithfield to Oxford Street, and it is almost as if he were a king communing with his subjects. In turn his novels are filled with the crowds of London, and are animated by the transience and the spectacle of street life.

Yet he liked to get out of London, too; his own experience of the city as prison had encouraged in him the tendency to wander far from the walls of old 'Babylon'. In 1837, the year that marked the final double number of *The Pickwick Papers*, he travelled down to Broadstairs and to Brighton. Broadstairs in

Above: Blackfriars viewed from Southwark Bridge.

particular became a favourite 'watering place', to use his own phrase for a resort that combined the twin attractions of privacy and the sea.

The sea was always important in Dickens's art, not least because his infant years had been spent in close proximity to the ports of southern England. Although he was pre-eminently an urban novelist, the sea is present in most of his work. It is the setting for Paul Dombey's lingering demise, for Mr Micawber's departure to unknown soils, and for Steerforth's death in the storm. The sea itself, like the crowds of London, acted as a natural aid to Dickens's imagination; it was as restless and unwearied as he was.

In this period, too, Dickens and Catherine made their first journey to the Continent, an experience they found sufficiently diverting to repeat on a number of occasions. France and Italy became akin to 'bolt-holes' for Dickens at times of tribulation or depression.

Above: Holborn Viaduct.

Yet the most significant journey was closer to home. Even as a child he had heard about the notorious 'Yorkshire schools'; perhaps he had feared that he might be sent to one. They advertised 'no vacations' and were the dumping ground for illegitimate or otherwise unwanted children; one schoolmaster, William Shaw, was tried and convicted for gross neglect of the small boys in his charge. It was a subject that, you might say, had been waiting for Dickens. After his assault upon the workings of the New Poor Law in the pages of *Oliver Twist*, it gave him the opportunity to raise the hammer of his wrath upon a further

abuse of children. All his intuitive sympathy, and all his repressed anger about his own treatment as a child, came to bear upon the little victims immured in Yorkshire.

He travelled up with his illustrator, 'Phiz', and visited Mr Shaw's establishment along with others in the neighbourhood. He wandered into the churchyard at Bowes, beside Shaw's Academy, and saw no fewer than thirty-four graves of dead scholars from schools in that vicinity. One tombstone read, 'Here lie the remains of GEORGE ASHTON TAYLOR' who 'died suddenly at Mr William Shaw's Academy of this place'. Dickens reported later that, on reading this inscription, the ghost of Smike entered his head – poor mistreated Smike, who moves like some piteous wraith through the pages of the novel and who might be some shadowy image of Dickens as a child.

Almost immediately on his return to London, he began *Nicholas Nickleby*; in one sense it marked a return to the picaresque narrative of *The Pickwick Papers*, with a large cast of itinerant characters, but into it Dickens poured all the harsh comedy of social suffering which had irradiated the pages of *Oliver Twist*. He knew now what it was to acquire power – power over the reader, certainly, but also power over the world. He had been attacked as a 'radical' in the established newspapers for his fulminations in *Oliver Twist*, but his exposure of the Yorkshire schools in *Nicholas Nickleby* led to the closure of many of them. The 'infant bastilles', in the words of one contemporary periodical, were quite exploded.

Above: Illustration from Nicholas Nickleby.

But the pages of *Nicholas Nickleby* are also filled with farce and humour; in the portraits of Mr Mantalini and Fanny Squeers, of Vincent Crummles and his redoubtable wife, the Gothic sufferings of the boys in Dotheboys Hall are complemented by grotesque laughter. Everything is of a piece.

Sir, My pa requests me to write to you, the doctors considering it doubtful whether he will ever recuvver the use of his legs which prevents his holding a pen...We were kimpelled to have him carried down into the kitchen where he now lays. You will judge from this that he has been brought very low...[Nicholas] assaulted my ma with dreadful violence, dashed her to the earth, and drove her back comb several inches into her head. A very little more and it must have entered her skull. We have a medical certifiket that if it had, the tortershell would have affected the brain.

Nicholas Nickleby, *Chapter XV, Fanny Squeers to Ralph Nickleby*

His attacks in no way diminished his popularity but, rather, served to heighten it. He was astonished to discover that the first serial number of *Nicholas Nickleby* had sold fifty thousand copies, more than any of the two previous novels, When the volume edition of *Oliver Twist* was published a little later, that too achieved an immense popular success; it had the distinction, also, of being the first book to include the words 'By Charles Dickens' on the title-page. His real name had at last been given to the world.

He had travelled down by steam train from Manchester to be present at the publication of *Oliver Twist* in volume form; he journeyed on the recently established railway line to London, and it is the first recorded journey ever made by Dickens on this new and powerful means of transportation. The railways were eventually to play a formidable and indeed fatal role in his life but, even at this early point, he understood their significance in the making

Above: The Lambeth Ragged School for Girls.

and shaping of the nation. At the time of the publication of *Oliver Twist* he was already in the middle of a tour of industrialized England. He wanted to see the new civilization. He travelled to Birmingham, to Manchester, to Wolverhampton, all the way observing 'miles of cinder-paths and blazing furnaces and roaring steam engines'.

In his own life, too, he represented all the energy and momentum of his period. He was always driving himself forward, so fast and so hard that he was sometimes concerned that his 'boiler' might 'burst'. So the railway train and he

were companions of the same intensely driven era. Dickens loved it. It was fast and punctual; it was a slave to time; it embodied energy and single-mindedness.

But there is another connection. The railway was also a commentary upon, and complement to, his own novels. It conjured up crowds, like those depicted in William Frith's painting *The Railway Station* and those that hurry through Dickens's fiction. The railways were considered to be a token of radical progress, not least because their extensions across London and the nation made visible for the first time the vast areas of poverty which had previously been the neglected or concealed face of nineteenth-century England. In the massive works of demolition undertaken to accommodate the railway lines, the regions of the poor were opened to other eyes just as surely as in *Oliver Twist*.

The world of Mr Pickwick was gone for ever. Euston Station was built in 1837, one of the years in which *The Pickwick Papers* was serialized, and was succeeded by Waterloo, King's Cross, Paddington, Victoria, Blackfriars, Charing Cross, St Pancras and Liverpool Street stations. The city that Dickens had known as a child was transformed.

Top: Bowes Hall School, the model for Dotheboys Hall in Nicholas Nickleby.
Above: Illustration from Nicholas Nickleby.

Thousands upon thousands of houses and public buildings were demolished. Streets and avenues were torn up. London was being rebuilt for the new age of speed and power. But if the city of his childhood was in the process of being extirpated, it continued to live in the pages of his fiction.

There is one other suggestive feature of his work in this period. He had agreed to edit and introduce the memoir of the most famous clown of the eighteenth and nineteenth centuries, Joseph Grimaldi, who almost single-handedly created the appearance of the pantomime. Dickens had always been interested in clowns and pantomimic illusion; even at the end of his life, he would enact the routine of the clown and pretend to tumble upon a blanket. But Grimaldi's memoir was by no means a comic narrative. It described hardship and weariness, endurance and illness. The fact that Dickens seems to have somehow identified himself with Grimaldi is plain in his account of the clown's ceaseless energy and almost unnatural exertions for the sake of his audience. But in a strange way Dickens seems to anticipate his own fate in his account of Grimaldi's 'premature old age and early decay'. He insists that Grimaldi's 'attention to his duties and invariable punctuality were always remarkable', again admiring the virtues he himself possessed, but then suggests that the 'immense fatigue' induced by over-work 'sowed the first

Above: The Victorian landscape accommodating the new railway line.

seeds of that extreme debility and utter prostration of strength from which, in the latter years of his life, he suffered so much'.

It should not be forgotten that Dickens was writing these words in the middle of a literary routine that included two novels, the proposal for a third, and endless disputes with publishers past and present in which his wilfulness always triumphed. In describing the fate of Grimaldi, he was outlining and predicting his own last years, but he did not seem able to make the connection. He did not understand himself at all or, rather, he did not wish to engage in any form of introspection or analysis; he simply wished to go ahead, to 'climb the mountain' as he used to say, and in the process he brushed aside any kind of misgiving.

He was now twenty-seven years old, and the enormous success of *Nicholas Nickleby* simply confirmed the popularity that he had acquired with *The Pickwick Papers* and *Oliver Twist*. 'What a face is his to meet in a drawing room,' Leigh Hunt wrote. 'It has the life and soul in it of fifty human beings.' Within his heart and imagination, too, Dickens nourished fifty human beings who emerge in the pages of his fiction as bright and as powerful as any people in the real world. He had already created Mr Pickwick, Sam Weller, Little Nell, Daniel Quilp, Dick Swiveller, Bob Sawyer, Mr Jingle, Oliver Twist, the Artful Dodger, Bill Sikes, Nancy, Fagin, Wackford Squeers, Nicholas Nickleby, Smike and a score of others. It is sometimes suggested that he merely created caricatures. But they are more like figures from eighteenth-century cartoons, where a single trait or characteristic is so extended that it takes on a life of its own; it represents a theatrical view of reality, perhaps, but one immeasurably deepened by Dickens's own art. The people *are* their behaviour, *are* their words, *are* their gestures; they inhabit some expansive world where the truth lies in appearances.

There is, however, another element of his strident characterization that merits reflection. In many instances he outlines one particular trait: Pecksniff is remarkable for his hypocrisy, for example, and Scrooge for his miserliness. Mr Micawber is memorable for his orotund phraseology, to the extent that he

Above: The maturing Dickens.

becomes his language; he is not an object of analysis or complex scrutiny. In that respect Dickens's figures are not moral beings but allegories; they impersonate or embody forces that are larger than themselves, and are filled with an almost impersonal power. That accounts for what may be called their hyper-reality and their absorbing interest.

Dickens was a master of locality as well as of character; in these first three novels he set the scene for much of his later work, whether it be in the energetic purlieus of Snow Hill or the squalid dens of Saffron Hill. It has been said that he created London for his contemporary audience, just as he fashioned its shape for later readers, and there is no doubt that within his pages a particular vision of dirtiness and decay will live for ever. It represents essentially the London that he had seen as a child; there are sketches in which he describes his infant wanderings through the city, and his almost clairvoyant sense of place derives from these earliest memories. His characters, too, might be said to derive from the fixed attention of a child's eyes.

The street was very narrow and mouldy, and the air was impregnated with filthy odours. There were a good many small shops; but the only stock in trade appeared to be heaps of children. . . The sole places that seemed to prosper amid the general blight of the place, were the public houses; and in them, the lowest orders of the Irish were wrangling with might and main. Covered ways and yards, which here and there diverged from the main street, disclosed little knots of houses, where drunken men and women were positively wallowing in filth.

Oliver Twist, *Chapter VIII*

Above: Session's House on Clerkenwell Green.

The external world, however, was continually moving forward. His father was once more accumulating debts on a grand scale. John Dickens had even gone so far as to borrow, or rather extort, money from his son's publishers – 'recollecting,' as he put it, 'how much your interests are bound up with those of my son'. Chapman and Hall had been pledged to secrecy, but of course the transactions were eventually revealed to Dickens; it also transpired that John Dickens had been selling his son's manuscripts and copies of his autograph. Dickens's reaction may be imagined rather than described. Certainly he reacted at whiplash speed. He travelled to Devon, rented a cottage, furnished it, and then ordered his parents down there – within a few days he had moved John and Elizabeth Dickens from London and had stowed them away like useless pieces of lumber in the countryside. He could not have acted more efficiently and effectively if he had been dispatching characters within a novel. Indeed, there is some suspicion that Dickens treated those around him just as if they had been part of a fictional narrative that he felt obliged to continue.

The strength of his will, however, had been immeasurably amplified by his success. He no longer considered publishers to be his employers; rather, he was employing them for the further advancement of his career, and all business relationships were obliged to reflect that fact. He engaged in difficult negotiations with Chapman and Hall, through the officious agency of John Forster, and came out with an agreement that promised him far greater profits and far more control. He had no sooner completed *Nicholas Nickleby* than he began to evolve the idea of a new fiction. He was the greatest novelist of his century, radiant with the fine blaze of his genius, but he was also an astute businessman who knew how to merchandise and market his wares. In later life he would identify himself with the 'cheap-jack' who sells trifling objects off the back of a cart, but he more closely resembled the managing director of a great and profitable concern.

Just as he had organized his parents, so now he proceeded to set the stage for the rest of his immediate family. Catherine had given birth to her third

child, Kate, and he realized that mother and children would require a house larger than that in Doughty Street; he also purchased a carriage for Catherine, perhaps in recompense for the sufferings she always endured at childbirth. After undergoing the miseries of house-hunting, he eventually settled on a property in Devonshire Terrace; it was much more lavishly furnished than its predecessor and, in particular, Dickens took great pains over its library. He did so for more than domestic reasons.

He was already being accused of Cockney 'ignorance', and of being quite outside the circles of history and philosophy. This was only partly true. He was a genius who picked up whatever knowledge or information he required before transforming it within the alembic of his imagination, but he had

Above: The streets of fashionable London.

decided to establish a library for himself which would encourage visitors to remark upon his extensive literary taste. He had become a figure in social and cultural circles, to be welcomed in the fashionable salons of Lady Holland and Samuel Rogers, and it had become necessary for him to 'live up' to his newly exalted status. Part of this was a kind of play-acting; he instinctively knew his worth and hardly needed to measure it against the inhabitants of London 'society', but he was always ready to don the appropriate costumes of the world. 'Mr Dickens' became a familiar figure, astonishingly young and colourfully dressed, who, despite his somewhat vivid appearance, preserved a calm demeanour and a modest deportment.

He also hosted parties and dinners in his new house; befitting a novelist who had celebrated the virtues of hospitality in his fiction, and had dwelled with relish upon plates heaped with sausages or pies, there was no shortage of food and drink in the Dickens household. Catherine Dickens even wrote a cookery book, under the supervision of her husband, in which the virtues of toasted cheese were rated very highly. Dickens's own abstemiousness has already been remarked; it is one of the curious aspects of his character that he was always generous to others but less than generous toward himself. It was part of his self-sufficiency, perhaps; it may also have been an aspect of his professionalism or practicality, which would allow nothing to impede his active progress in the world.

There was one other visitor at Devonshire Terrace; it was a pet raven, named Grip, whose feats of daring and chicanery were chronicled by Dickens in letters to his friends. His untimely death was mourned in a characteristic fashion: 'On the clock striking twelve he appeared slightly agitated, but he soon recovered, walked twice or thrice along the coach-house, stopped to bark, staggered, exclaimed Halloa old girl (his favourite expression), and died.' Dickens promptly acquired another bird of the same species and his partiality for it prompted the artist Edwin Landseer to dub him 'raven mad'.

Above: Dickens's children Charley, Mamey, Katey and Walter with the pet raven.

The remark is said to have circulated with unhappy consequences, since it was then rumoured that Dickens was indeed 'raving mad'; there were even reports that he had been confined to an asylum. It is one of the disadvantages of genius, especially one that expresses itself in copious and rapid composition, that it may seem perilously close to insanity; there were many people who simply could not believe that a young man could produce such extraordinary works without in some way damaging his mind.

He was always considered to be an 'odd' person; as his school companions had observed many years before, for example, he was prone to 'immoderate laughter'. But this was only one feature of a generally extravagant and nervous personality. His reaction to the marriage of Queen Victoria and Prince Albert is in that respect typical. He professed to be madly in love with the young queen, and in letters bewailed what he considered to be a personal

Above: Devonshire Terrace, London.

abandonment. 'The presence of my wife aggravates me. I loathe my parents. I detest my house. I begin to have thoughts of the Serpentine, of the Regent's Canal, of the razors upstairs, of the chemist's down the street, of poisoning myself…' And so it goes on, in a litany of comic despair. And of course in one sense he did loathe his parents, and Catherine did aggravate him. Even in a moment of farce, he could not help but reveal his true nature. He himself was aware of his oddity; he sometimes claimed to be 'afraid of myself', as if he sensed that the power of feeling within him might be too strong for him to control. His only relief, then, was in writing.

That potent combination, of strong emotion and compulsive composition, was nowhere more evident than in the novel that he had recently begun. As part of his new arrangement with Chapman and Hall, his publishers, he had agreed to edit a new weekly periodical; it was entitled *Master Humphrey's Clock*, and would consist of papers and essays that 'Master Humphrey' had discovered in the clock itself. The sales of the first number were very high, but then fell off when the public discovered that this was not a new novel from Dickens after all, but a miscellany of unrelated items. Dickens realized at once that only his fiction could save the enterprise, and he began work upon what he termed a 'little child story' to which he gave the title *The Old Curiosity Shop*. It concerned the doomed wanderings of Little Nell and her grandfather, escaping from the depredations of a threatening dwarf named Quilp, and at once it captured the public imagination.

There was something of an obsession with thwarted or threatened innocence in nineteenth-century England, primarily because it represented an overwhelming and unsettling reality; the number of child prostitutes in the streets, and of child labourers in the mines and factories, was a terrible indictment of Victorian 'civilization', which seemed to have built upon the

Above: Little Nell, the doomed heroine of The Old Curiosity Shop.

shuddering backs of oppressed innocents. So as Dickens continued with his tale of Little Nell's suffering, not unilluminated by passages of wild humour and grotesque pantomimic farce, there were many thousands of readers who were so immensely touched and saddened by the pathos of the young girl's wanderings that they begged the novelist to grant her a kindly fate.

Not the least of those affected was Dickens himself. He was driving forward the narrative to the point of Little Nell's death, but the spectacle of her imminent demise seemed to unnerve him as thoroughly as any of his readers. 'All night I have been pursued by the child,' he wrote to a friend, 'and this morning I am unrefreshed and miserable.' He alludes here to a disquieting phenomenon about which he often spoke; his characters talked to him, and sometimes touched him. They were so real that there were occasions when he could literally hear and see them. This is perhaps what is meant by the adage that genius is, indeed, close to madness. 'I am slowly murdering that poor child,' he wrote, 'and grow wretched over it. It wrings my heart.

Yet it must be.' The idea of murdering a child is perhaps an unpleasant one, but the emotional identification of Dickens with his story was so strong that even the most unhappy impulses play a part.

When the death came, it is not too much to say that an entire nation mourned. It is well known that eminent men, such as Judge Jeffreys, broke down and wept on reading the fatal instalment. The Irish statesman Daniel O'Connell threw the periodical out of the carriage of a speeding train and exclaimed, 'He should not have killed her!' Much has been written about the reticence and coldness of the Victorian male but, in truth, nineteenth-century Englishmen and Englishwomen were more susceptible to tears than their modern counterparts. There was a ready emotionalism in a society capable of great pity as well as great cruelty and neglect. And yet the Victorians were weeping over the conditions that they had created. They were weeping for themselves.

Above: A child trapper in the Lancashire and Cheshire coal pits.

'She is sleeping soundly,' he said, 'but no wonder. Angel hands have strewn the ground deep with snow, that the lightest footstep may be lighter yet; and the very birds are dead, that they may not wake her. She used to feed them, sir. Though never so cold and hungry, the timid things would fly from us. They never flew from her!'

The Old Curiosity Shop, *Chapter LXXI*

The full flood of Dickens's feeling entered his next novel, which was also serialized in *Master Humphrey's Clock. Barnaby Rudge* is set in the period of the Gordon Riots of 1780, a carnival of violence on the streets of London when the capital came perilously close to mob rule. The demonstrations were ostensibly against legislation freeing Roman Catholics of certain restrictions, but quickly the rage for disorder consumed the crowds. In the novel Dickens dramatized these scenes with great gusto; there was an element of ferocity within him which identified with mayhem and sympathized with the rioters against the established order. Poor half-witted Barnaby is himself incarcerated in Newgate, placed in a strong stone cell and fettered with irons; it is one of the enduring images of Dickens's fiction. 'I have just burnt into Newgate,' he told Forster. 'I feel quite smoky when I am at work.' He could be a thoroughly angry man, even if that anger was originally provoked by visions of his own childhood neglect.

The gutters of the street, and every crack and fissure on the stones, ran with scorching spirit, which being dammed up by busy hands, overflowed the road and pavement, and formed a great pool, into which the people dropped down dead by dozens. While some stooped with their lips to the brink, and never raised their heads again, others sprang up from the fiery draught, and danced, half in mad triumph, and half in the agony of suffocation, until they fell, and steeped their corpses in the liquor that had killed them.

Barnaby Rudge, *Chapter LXVIII*

Barnaby Rudge, like its immediate predecessor, was conceived and written in weekly instalments. Dickens was such a consummate professional that he easily mastered the new regimen of work, even though he sometimes felt the small space to be 'crushing'; in these novels there is no diminution in the quality of his prose, which, as a register of impassioned feeling, is unequalled in its power and its intensity. He was of course a master of comic dialogue, where an entire character can be measured in an unforgettable phrase, but he was also adept at conveying the pathos and suffering of the world in cadences that are very much like those of nineteenth-century poetry. He was, in Oscar Wilde's memorable phrase, a lord of language.

He might almost have been a lord of the real world also. In the summer of 1841, in his twenty-ninth year, he went on what can only be called a triumphal progress through Scotland. He told Forster after his arrival that 'the hotel is perfectly besieged' and 'I have been forced to take refuge in a sequestered apartment'. Amidst scenes such as this he began to understand the measure of his fame. In Edinburgh he was entertained at a great dinner, and was hailed by what he called 'enthoosemoosy'; nevertheless he stated that he remained 'as cool as a cucumber', an uninteresting phrase about an interesting condition of restraint or reticence. He never did react to signs of rejoicing in his presence and, in general circumstances, he always managed to keep his reactions under stern control. This in no sense derived from absence of feeling but, rather, from the opposite: his temperament was a nervous and excessive one, and reserve was the only way of disciplining his nature.

The wildness of his true self emerges, however, in the descriptions of his journey through the Scottish Highlands, where he dilates upon the desolation of moors and the magnificence of mountains; he loved storms and all extravagant natural phenomena, too, as if somehow they reflected his own excess and

Top: The exercise yard at Newgate Prison.
Above: Illustration of Barnaby Rudge in Newgate Prison.

turbulence. But he also remained thoroughly professional, and sent back to London the weekly instalments of *Barnaby Rudge*. He was well aware of his vocation. At one stage of his travels, for example, a Scottish county asked him to become their member of Parliament; he refused, as he had done with such requests in the past, since he knew instinctively that he was not suited to political life in any of its current manifestations.

After the tumult of Scotland, he and his wife retired to the relative sobriety of Broadstairs in Kent, now their favourite 'seaside' resort, where Dickens indulged in his usual routine of writing and sea-bathing during the day, with games and dances in the evening. He was joined by his siblings and parents, who had been temporarily summoned from Devon, as well as assorted acquaintances who were forced to indulge his high spirits. One guest, a certain 'Eleanor P.', left a memoir of her visit in which she dwelled upon the peculiarities of Dickens's behaviour; he was often seized with a wild hilarity, on one occasion seizing her and practically plunging her into the sea, which could be followed by taciturnity and even unfriendliness. She noted that the members of his family seemed to be afraid of him and wary of his moods; they knew him only too well.

His publishers, too, understood the power of his will. Through the agency of Forster he informed them that he wished to leave off his writing for a year; he had visited Sir Walter Scott's mansion in Edinburgh, and had become uneasily aware of that novelist's unhappy last years in which he literally wrote himself to death. For the last six years Dickens himself had been constantly engaged in fiction – sometimes, as we have seen, writing two novels at the same time – and he feared that Scott's fate might be visited upon his own career. He wanted to stop. Also, he wanted to get away.

Passengers disembarking at New York Harbour had been greeted by the enquiry: 'Is Little Nell dead?' It was also reported that cowboys had read the adventures of the poor young girl around their camp fires. The American

Above: Barnaby Rudge.

writer Washington Irving had written to inform Dickens that, if he travelled to the United States, 'it would be a triumph for me [Dickens] from one end of the States to the other, as was never known in any nation'. As soon as he had conceived the idea, it became a pressing reality to be fulfilled as soon as practic-able. The objections of Catherine were immaterial; she cried every time her husband brought up the matter, but he persisted in his determination. She must go with him and, what is more, she must enjoy herself; as he said, 'it must be a source of happiness to her' even if she was obliged to leave her children and travel for several months through unknown regions.

He had already purchased many books on America, and determined that he would add to their number with a benevolent account of the country. Already in his imagination he had limned the outline of an ideal republic, free and egalitarian, which had released itself from the conventionalities of the 'old world'.

There was one small matter, however, that had to be resolved before his departure; he discovered that the excessive hours sitting at his desk had provoked a fistula or growth through the rectal wall. It could only be removed by surgery, and the agonizing operation was performed without anaesthetic; the pain must have been almost unbearable, as the tissue was cut away and the rectal wall stitched up, but Dickens steeled himself for this ordeal as he did for every other decisive moment in his life.

He was obliged to recuperate on a sofa for several days, with Catherine taking dictation from him, but still he managed to complete the final episodes of *Barnaby Rudge*. Within a short period he was as active and busy as ever, and was soon engaged in a frantic round of 'farewell' visits and dinners. Every second thought was now of America.

Above: The Dickens's favourite 'seaside' resort – Broadstairs, Kent.

CHAPTER FOUR

Dickens in America

Charles and Catherine Dickens set sail on the steamship *Britannia* in the first week of 1842; their cabin was pitifully small, by Dickens's report, with a bed the size of a muffin and pillows the size of crumpets. The crossing was impeded by violent storms, among the worst seen upon the Atlantic for some years, but Dickens tried to keep up the spirits of his wife and servant by playing tunes on an accordion; he was once more 'as cool as a cucumber', despite the ferocity of the weather. Indeed, in some sense storms were truly Dickens's element. He revelled in fury.

When the *Britannia* eventually berthed in Halifax, Nova Scotia, he was dragged off to the local assembly by its Speaker. 'I wish you could have seen

Above: The Britannia *in Boston harbour.*
Opposite: Washington DC.

the crowds cheering the inimitable in the streets,' he wrote later to Forster. 'I wish you could have seen judges, law-officers, bishops, and law-makers welcoming the inimitable.' It was the first time he had used the phrase in description of himself, but 'the inimitable' seems an appropriate nickname for a young novelist who was receiving such an extraordinary reception thousands of miles away from home.

From Halifax the *Britannia* sailed down the coast to Boston, and arrived in that town's harbour a little less than three weeks after its departure from Liverpool. The welcome for Dickens was once again overwhelming. When he was taken to the State House, crowds filled the street to cheer his progress.

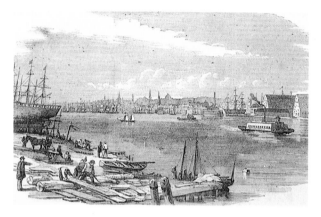

When he attended a local theatre, the audience stood to cheer him nine times. An innumerable stream of visitors besieged him in his hotel, and he received so many letters and invitations that he was obliged to hire a secretary to answer them. When he visited one artist's studio, the number of people waiting to see him became so great that he was obliged to lock himself in one of the rooms. On other occasions pieces of his coat were snipped away by hunters after literary memorabilia. 'I can give you no conception of my welcome here,' he wrote to a friend. 'There never was a king or emperor upon the earth so cheered and followed by crowds…'

Like some king or emperor, too, he was taken on tours of the public institutions of Boston. Dickens was particularly interested in visiting the House of Correction and the Hospital for the Insane, in order to see how American methods of punishment and control compared with those of his own country. His interest in the extremes of the human condition was easily married to the professional inclinations of a born journalist. He was impressed by the systems of the 'new world', and made detailed observations which he later worked up in his account of his travels. He was intrigued by the factories and mills of the region, too, where a kind of paternal discipline gained his full approval. For such an enthusiastic celebrant of family life, paternalism was the ultimate standard of political and social mores.

The welcome for Dickens was no less warm in Hartford and New Haven, where he was serenaded by the students of Yale University. In New York he was

Top: Boston Harbour.
Above: Boston State House, Massachusetts.

once more surrounded by crowds, fêted at dinners and balls, and generally lionized within an inch of his life. There was a great 'Boz Ball' in New York, when tableaux from his novels were mounted around the assembly room, and a few days later a 'Dickens Dinner' was attended by hundreds of his admirers.

There were some, however, who were not lost in admiration. He was considered by the more genteel in American 'society' to be a little vulgar; his clothing was considered too 'flashy' and his manner too 'showy'. He was described as a typical Cockney, who even had the temerity to comb his hair at a dinner party. But the most vociferous criticism arose out of references, in one of his speeches, to the matter of international copyright. His work was being pirated and published in America without any authorization and,

more importantly, without any payment. When he complained about the matter, however, the newspapers accused him of being opportunistic and greedy. Since the same newspapers were the greatest literary pirateers and profiteers, they might be suspected of prejudice in the matter.

But Dickens was not to be cowed by editorials. He insisted on raising the issue on almost every public occasion; as the opposition to his pronouncements grew, so did his anger. 'My blood so boiled as I thought of the monstrous injustice,' he wrote, 'that I felt as if I were twelve feet high when I thrust it down their throats.' It ought to be remembered here that Dickens was relatively short in stature, and was sometimes referred to as 'the little man'; one consequence of his rhetorical power may have been his own sense that he had grown in height when he expatiated on his most powerful feelings.

Above: The Tombs — the detention centre in New York.

Individual Americans whom he encountered, however, manifested nothing but courtesy and kindness. He struck up friendships with the two leading writers of the age, Washington Irving and Henry Wadsworth Longfellow; Irving in particular supported his demands for international copyright, and signed a petition in its favour. Yet his experiences over the issue encouraged grave doubts about the nature of American society itself, where it was not considered politic to contradict the newspapers or to challenge the whole system of mercantile arrangements upon which that society was based. 'I do fear,' he wrote, 'that the heaviest blow ever dealt at liberty will be dealt by this country, in the failure of its example to the earth.'

He had come, he thought, to encounter a young and optimistic republic, but the reality had fallen far short of his expectations. After two or three weeks in New York, for example, his first favourable impressions of Massachusetts and Connecticut were being replaced by a more dismal and disillusioned sense of American life. His visit to the 'low' areas of the city, and to its central prison, known as the Tombs, convinced him that life for the poor was no different from, and in certain respects a great deal worse than, that in London. 'The Five Points', a district at the centre of one of New York's most impoverished areas, was equivalent to the Seven Dials near Covent Garden.

What! Do you thrust your common offenders against the police discipline of the town, into such holes as these? Do men and women, against whom no crime is proved, lie here all night in perfect darkness, surrounded by the noisome vapours which encircle that flagging lamp you light us with, and breathing this filthy and offensive stench! Why, such indecent and disgusting dungeons as these cells, would bring disgrace upon the most despotic empire in the world!

American Notes for General Circulation, *Chapter VI*

Above: Washington Irving.

He was also growing tired of the excessive public attention. 'If I turn into the street,' he complained, 'I am followed by a multitude…I get out at a station, and can't drink a glass of water, without having a hundred people looking down my throat when I open my mouth to swallow.' Dickens had neither time nor opportunity for those precious periods of self-communing in which he refreshed his imagination, those periods of solitary and silent thought in which he reclaimed possession of himself. Catherine was herself now feeling the strain of the protracted tour, and in particular missed the presence of her children. But their travels continued. The battle, in one of Dickens's characteristic phrases, had to be fought out.

So the two of them, together with their servant Anne, travelled further south to Philadelphia and then to Washington. Dickens found the trains unbearably hot, and the American habit of spitting at every available opportunity quite disconcerting. He noted of one journey that the flashes of saliva out of one railway car 'flew so perpetually and incessantly out of their windows all the way, that it looked as though they were ripping open feather-beds inside, and letting the wind dispose of the feathers'. This is a good example of Dickens's remarkably comic gift of observation, where a commonplace reality is viewed in a fantastic light. In Philadelphia he met Edgar Allan Poe, whose manner charmed Dickens into a promise that he would help with the English publication of Poe's eerie stories; in Washington he met the President of the United States, John Tyler, who remarked: 'I am astonished to see so young a man, Sir.' This was indeed by now a familiar response and, since there did not seem much else to say, Dickens soon rose to end the interview.

Top: President John Tyler, 10th President of the USA.
Above: Philadelphia Harbour.

He was more voluble in his letters, however, where he railed against the practice of slavery in the Southern States as abominable in itself and destructive to slaves and slave-owners alike. Under the circumstances, it was perhaps inevitable that he would now be playing 'Home Sweet Home' on the accordion each night. He had come to recognize the fact that he was thoroughly English in temperament and behaviour, 'with a yearning after our English customs and our English manners'; it was not the least of his self-discoveries in the course of his journey, and one that had wider applications for his art. He began now to understand the native sources of his genius as a gift rather than as a limitation.

He had by now concluded that he wished to avoid any public engagements for the rest of his journey, so he and Catherine now behaved very much like individuals on a private tour. When they arrived in Pennsylvania they took a canal boat on which they were obliged to share cabins with their fellow travellers. Dickens himself was not impressed by the Americans in his company, the vast majority of whom he regarded as intolerable bores, but he tried in his usual fashion to make light of a difficult situation. He cracked jokes and acted in his facetious and 'Cockney' manner. The Americans were astonished to discover his preoccupation with cleanliness and fitness, however, particularly when he jumped from the boat on to the towpath and proceeded to walk for five or six miles at a stretch. He had such superfluous energy that he had to expend it in any way he could.

On steamboats they embarked upon the Ohio river, later making their way upon the Mississippi, and Dickens was struck by the wildness and desolation of the landscapes through which they passed; he would later revive them in the American scenes of *Martin Chuzzlewit*. This was a primeval wilderness indeed, and Catherine was fearful about rumours of Indians in the vicinity. When they arrived in St Louis, Missouri, however, they were greeted

Above: Edgar Allan Poe.

by educated and practical people – among them a Unitarian minister, William Greenleaf Eliot, who is perhaps best known now for being the grandfather of T.S. Eliot. (T.S. Eliot himself was born and raised in St Louis, so what Dickens considered to be a wilderness could bear strange fruit.) This was the most western stage of their travels, celebrated in a visit to the prairies, by which Dickens was distinctly underwhelmed, and from Missouri they travelled to Cincinnati and Columbus. In Cleveland Dickens happened to read a newspaper article excoriating the English, and so he refused to see the mayor who was waiting in attendance. In the same town he was victim to literary sightseers who looked stolidly in through the window of their little cabin 'while I was washing and Kate lay in bed'. After the melancholy waste-lands of the riverine states, however, he travelled excitedly towards Niagara. Here once again was a natural phenomenon that seemed worthy of Dickens, and he dilated upon the ferocity and majesty of its endless cascades.

The Dickens party took one last journey and in May arrived in Canada; that country seemed to be better suited to Dickens than the United States, principally because of the reserve or reticence of its citizens. They were more English, in other words. Now that they were close to the end of their American adventure, every third thought of Dickens was of home.

In Montreal he held a reunion with the Earl of Mulgrave, whom he had met on the tempestuous voyage across the Atlantic, and promised to arrange some amateur theatricals for a local charity. He agreed to be stage manager and principal actor – both of which roles he had been playing for most of his life – and at once set to frantic work. 'Everybody was told they would have to submit to the most iron despotism,' he told Forster; this was no idle threat, and he dragooned a motley collection of amateurs into something like professional shape. Even Catherine Dickens was given a part and, much to her husband's amazement, carried if off with some distinction.

Above: Henry Wadsworth Longfellow.

The time for their departure was approaching, and Dickens made the arrangements to travel back to New York. Before going on board he made one last excursion to visit a Shaker village in New York State; he was distinctly unimpressed by their brand of moral rigour and drew effective caricatures of that pious group in his book of American travels. Ostentatious moralism never did appeal to him; it smacked of cant or hypocrisy, all the worse for manifesting itself in such drab circumstances.

And then, on 7 June 1842, six months after their arrival in the United States, Charles and Catherine Dickens boarded the sailing ship *George Washington* for their return to England. He had chosen sail over steam on this occasion, since the experience of fire and smoke on the outward journey had persuaded him of the relative safety of the older form of transport. It was one of the few times when Dickens deliberately avoided the appurtenances of 'contemporary' life. His heart and imagination were in the early nineteenth century, but his observations were always those of a 'progressive' interested in modern technologies and products.

On the journey back he seems to have fallen victim to a prolonged bout of hysterical hilarity. With two other passengers he started a 'United Vagabonds' club; they dressed up as Dickensian characters, and all three of them pretended to be doctors curing other voyagers with scissors and paste. At best their antics anticipated those of the Marx Brothers, with Dickens in the role of Groucho; at worst they might be regarded as sufficiently childish not to require comment. It is interesting and significant, however, that the mid-Victorians could indeed become 'childish' with very little prompting; it has something to do with that innocence which they believed they had lost (memorialized, of course, in *The Old Curiosity Shop*), but it is connected as well with that ready emotionalism which was one of their most striking and attractive characteristics.

The return of Charles and Catherine Dickens to London,
after three weeks at sea, is an appropriate indication of that
fullness or floridity of feeling. When Forster heard that
Dickens was waiting for him in a carriage, he rushed out of
the house and, seated next to his friend, began to cry. All
the Dickens children had surrendered to various forms of
hysteria, and young Charley fell into convulsions for which
a doctor had to be summoned. There was a grand reunion
dinner at Greenwich, at which various eminent parties
became gloriously drunk.

Yet even as he celebrated his return Dickens was already
preparing memoranda for an American travel book to be
entitled *American Notes for General Circulation*; he had brought back
a number of newspapers and magazines, perhaps to refresh his
memory of their enormities, and borrowed the letters that he had written to
friends during the course of his journey. Out of these he concocted a narrative
that is observant and jocose in equal measure. It begins with a comic account of
the sea-crossing, and ends with a short disquisition on public health; Dickens's
own adventures are not allowed to obtrude, and there is instead a sober account
of the various penal and medical institutions of the country. There are also
sharp remonstrances upon the ubiquity of spitting and the iniquity of the slave
trade. The response of the American press was perhaps predictable. Already
there had been a headline announcing that 'DICKENS IS A FOOL, AND A
LIAR'. In its review of the book itself the *New York Herald* maintained that Dickens
had 'the most coarse, vulgar, impudent and superficial mind…that ever had
the courage to write about this original and remarkable country'. Enough said.

Yet he still enjoyed the most cordial relations with individual Americans.
Longfellow visited England soon after Dickens's return, and at once Dickens
led him on a frenzied round of dinners and parties. He also asked Longfellow
to accompany him on less salubrious expeditions through the poorer parts of

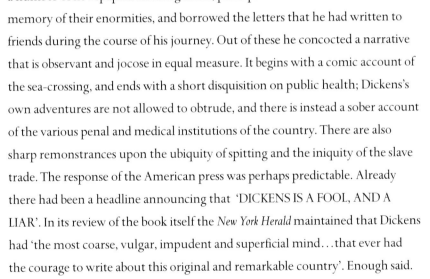

Above and opposite: Dickens as he appeared to the American press — impudent and vulgar.

CHURCH LANE
BLOOMSBURY

London. He took him to lodging houses and tenement slums, almost as if
he were showing him both the sources of his inspiration and the roots of
his genius. The conditions were so foul, however, that when one of their
companions on these nocturnal exploits was about to enter a boarding house
– or, rather, a long room with stale mattresses in it – he was promptly sick at
the smells that issued from it.

After Longfellow had returned to his own country Dickens ventured
upon a more healthful expedition to Cornwall where, he informed a friend,
'I never laughed in my life as I did on this journey. It would have done you
good to hear me.' Dickens was always convinced of the curative properties of
his personality, often acting as a doctor to friends in need, and this innocent
vanity is all part of his excessive and overflowing energy. 'I do believe there

Above: Bloomsbury, one of the London slums visited by Dickens.

never was such a trip,' he wrote in characteristically
Dickensian manner. Throughout his life he dealt in
superlative and hyperbole. There never was such a
dinner. There never was such a speech. There never
was such a reception. It is related to his own extrava-
gance in the world, of course, but it may also reflect a
native Cockney passion for over-statement.

Dickens began 1843 by performing as a conjuror
at a Twelfth Night party, but a more significant feat of
prestidigitation was about to begin. He started work
upon a new novel. Yet first he had to find a name. He
considered Sweezleden and Sweezlewag, Chuzzletoe
and Chubblewig, before eventually encountering
Martin Chuzzlewit in all his glory. This was to be a novel
concerned with the machinations of selfishness, with

Pecksniff as its prime and hypocritical mover, and he pursued it through a year
where he saw the elements of selfishness everywhere. The owners of the mills
and factories had been complaining that the 'reformers' of working conditions,
especially those for children, were guilty of curtailing the commercial greatness
of England. The opponents of public sanitation argued that the immemorial
rights of parishes and vestries would be thrown away in this rush towards
unnecessary legislation. Dickens read reports on both subjects and corresponded with the reformer Southwood Smith on the necessity for some kind of
polemical statement. 'When you see what I do,' he wrote, '…you will certainly
feel that a sledge-hammer blow has come down…'

There was rampant cant and selfishness, too, in the self-congratulatory
speeches of businessmen and clergymen. He was obliged to attend one such
public dinner and later excoriated the 'sleek, slobbering, bow-paunched, over-
fed, apoplectic snorting cattle' who dined on the sufferings of the poor. In the
course of his fury he visited several institutions for the rescue of those who

Above: The tea-party in Martin Chuzzlewit.

had been trodden down in the battle of life. He was particularly struck by the 'ragged schools' of London where the indigent children were somehow persuaded to attend classes for the most elementary learning. 'I have very seldom seen,' he wrote, 'in all the strange and dreadful things I have seen in London and elsewhere, anything so shocking as the dire neglect of soul and body exhibited among these children.' He laid these things in his heart, from which they eventually burst out in some of the most impassioned prose he ever wrote.

He was also beset by distress, or at least disappointment, closer to home. His parents were complaining about their relative exile in Devon, while his brothers were reduced to the position of family retainers. Fred, in particular, was running up debts that he seemed to expect his older brother to repay. Yet out of his outrage, and anger, sprang Dickens's comedy. The first episodes of *Martin Chuzzlewit* are some of the funniest he had ever written. Pecksniff makes his appearance with his two daughters, Mercy and Charity – 'Not unholy names, I hope?' – and the grotesque Mrs Gamp emerges into a world that has never quite forgotten her.

'I think, young woman,' said Mrs Gamp to the assistant chambermaid, in a tone expressive of weakness, 'that I could pick a little bit of pickled salmon, with a nice little sprig of fennel, and a sprinkling of white pepper... In case there should be such a thing as a cowcumber in the 'ouse, will you be so kind as bring it, for I'm rather partial to 'em, and they does a world of good in a sick room. If they draws the Brighton Old Tippler here, I takes that ale at night, my love; it being considered wakeful by the doctors. And whatever you do, young woman, don't bring more than a shilling's worth of gin and water-warm when I rings the bell a second time; for that is always my allowance, and I never takes a drop beyond!'

Martin Chuzzlewit, *Chapter XXV*

Above: Classes in a London Ragged School.

The sales of the novel, however, were not keeping pace with its author's inventions. The fifth number had a circulation of only twenty thousand, some eighty thousand less than its immediate predecessor, and Dickens was obliged to take action. Since *American Notes* had been a success, he decided that he must send Martin Chuzzlewit in the same direction that he had gone.

The hero would travel to America, there to receive as many rebuffs and misadventures as Dickens himself. It was a sudden, though not an incautious, decision. In fact the change of plot caused a greater sensation in America than it did in England; in a New York theatre, during a production of *Macbeth*, the offending novel was thrown into the witches' cauldron to prolonged applause and cheering.

Yet the sales in England were still not rising at any great rate, and his publishers foolishly mentioned the fact that there was a repayment clause in his contract by means of which they could reduce his income if sales were not meeting his advance. He was so angry with them that, immediately, he conceived schemes to lay them aside and to find some other publishing outlet. He had recently helped to establish a Society of Authors and, as his campaign on the subject of international copyright had proved, he was fierce in pursuit of what he considered to be his 'rights'.

Above: Martin Chuzzlewit.

The bad sales, however, were a source of great anxiety. He needed to earn more money. He needed to earn it quickly. It was at this moment of crisis that the idea of a 'Christmas book' first occurred to him. *A Christmas Carol* was conceived when Dickens attended a meeting of the Manchester Athenaeum, a club devoted to the educational aspirations of working men. He made a speech in which he touched upon the evils bred by ignorance as 'the parent of misery and crime', and emphasized the pressing need for all classes of English society to work together for the common good. It was an effective speech, as all of his perorations were, and he came back to London with the germ of an idea. It was an idea in which the figures of Scrooge, of Bob Cratchit, of Tiny Tim and the ghosts of Christmas were all mysteriously combined.

He set to work at once, and the strange story of haunting and greed took such possession of him that he 'wept, and laughed, and wept again'. He took walks of twenty miles through the night streets of London, refreshing and replenishing himself with great draughts of city atmosphere. He was deeply affected by the narrative because it addressed his own most secret desires and fears. He had in part written it for money, in a period when he was busy warding off financial demands from his relatives. The infancy of Scrooge, too, is uncannily like that of Dickens; the miser has a beloved sister named Fan and is haunted by the figures of his childhood reading in the shape of Ali Baba and Robinson Crusoe's parrot. In a sense Scrooge is a phantom of Charles Dickens. However exaggerated a self-portrait, he is touched with the energy and brightness of the novelist himself. That is why he has lived in the popular imagination for 150 years.

Everyone now remembers the miser, together with Tiny Tim, but for Dickens the two principal figures of the story were the phantoms of Ignorance and Want that are shown to Scrooge. He called it a 'little tract

Above: Scene from A Christmas Carol.

for the times'; so did the whole nation. This was the secret of his power. His needs corresponded with the needs of his age. His desires corresponded with the desires of the age. His hopes corresponded with the hopes of his age. In the phantoms of Ignorance and Want he glimpsed his own helpless and hopeless childhood, but he saw also the outline of Victorian civilization.

'Spirit! Are they yours?' Scrooge could say no more.

'They are Man's,' said the Spirit, looking down upon them. 'And they cling to me, appealing from their fathers. This boy is Ignorance. This girl is Want. Beware them both, and all of their degree, but most of all beware this boy, for on his brow I see that written which is Doom, unless the writing be erased.'

A Christmas Carol, *Stave Three*

He told Forster that 'I feel my power now, more than I ever did'. But that power brought him neither contentment nor self-sufficiency. He felt threatened and embattled. The success of *A Christmas Carol* had been so great that a pirated version appeared in a periodical. In the past Dickens had ignored all these tributes to his art, considering imitation to be the flattery that mediocrity paid to genius, but in his sensitive state he decided to sue the writer and publisher. He won the case convincingly, but the other parties arranged for a discreet bankruptcy. Dickens could not even recover his costs. The legal venture had cost him approximately £700. He never went to the courts again on the matter of literary piracy.

His discomfiture was increased when the profits of *A Christmas Carol* were revealed. The sales had been large indeed, but the costs of producing a somewhat luxurious volume were even larger. He had hoped to make £1000 from the 'little tract', but in fact he had earned less than a quarter of that sum. He reacted with all the nervous excitability of his nature. 'Such a night as I have passed!' he wrote on receiving the news. 'I really believed I should never get up again, until I had passed through all the horrors of a fever.' The fever was caused by prospects of poverty, of course, since it was the one single fate he had tried to exorcise all of his life.

He also professed to believe that, if he did not reduce his expenditure, 'I shall be ruined past all mortal hope of redemption'. This was an over-statement in Dickens's familiar style, but the anxiety and horror behind his words cannot be over-stated. The remembrance of his childhood helplessness and penury had never left him and, in this difficult situation, it was as if he were slipping back into a dreadful past.

He felt trapped on every side. His parents and siblings were making continual demands upon him, and Catherine now gave birth to their fifth child. Of the baby, he wrote, 'I decline (on principle) to look at the latter object', but the comedy may be felt to conceal some latent hostility to the sight of another burden upon his purse. So he was restless, with ideas of flight from England. He considered Italy, France and Germany as possible destinations. The success of *American Notes* emboldened him to consider another travel book. He was always looking forward.

Opposite: A scene from A Christmas Carol.
Above: Scrooge's third visitor.

CHAPTER FIVE

European adventures

Beneath his powerful yet understandable ambitions and desires, Dickens seemed to possess some incurable need to fly from ordinary reality altogether. If it did not meet his great expectations, then it must be moulded into another shape. It accounts for his earnest desire to travel to new scenes and new people, but it also lies behind his predilection for acting and for his furious immersion in his fictions.

After much consultation and contemplation Dickens had decided that he and his family should spend a year in Italy, and arrangements were made for the rental of an old house in Genoa. Before his departure, however, he had to fulfil speaking engagements in Birmingham and Liverpool, on both occasions on behalf of educational institutions for working people. It was the cause perhaps closest to him, and one with which he no doubt associated his own bitter sorrow at the sudden loss of schooling. He wrote to a friend about his conduct at Birmingham, 'Sir, he was jocular, pathetic, eloquent, conversational, illustrative, and wise – always wise.' Whether this may be regarded as a token of his vanity, or of his farcical humour, is difficult to determine.

There was a curious incident at Liverpool, however, which throws an interesting light upon his character. He encountered a young woman, Christiana Weller, who bore a striking resemblance to his sister-in-law, Mary Hogarth.

Opposite: Genoa, Italy.

Eighteen years old, she was only a year older than the age at which Mary had died in Dickens's arms. Immediately he seems to have fallen into some kind of passionate delirium. He glimpsed an 'angel's message in her face…that smote me to the heart'. She was a 'spiritual young creature' and one 'destined to an early death, I fear'. He could not cease thinking about her and, if the circumstances had been different, he swore that he would have married her.

It is a puzzling episode largely because of Dickens's forthrightness about the matter. He could no more conceal his feelings than he could stop

breathing. He seems to have been totally unaware of any pattern to his infatuations – that he seemed temperamentally unable to resist the allure of young women, such as Mary Hogarth, on their way to an 'early death'. They must die because they must be innocent of any sexuality. His love was therefore purified by dwelling upon their mortality. It is equally characteristic, however, that he lost all interest in Miss Weller after her unexpected marriage.

For the forthcoming journey to Italy Dickens purchased a great carriage with which to transport Catherine, five children and three servants – together with Catherine's sister Georgina, who was now an integral part of the household in her role as companion to Catherine and unofficial nurse to the children. A few days before he embarked upon his continental adventure, Dickens and friends held a celebration dinner at Greenwich to mark the final number of *Martin Chuzzlewit*; it is worth remarking upon the occasion, if only because the painter Turner was one of the guests. He, too, was a Cockney visionary who saw in London all the symbolic powers of the world.

Finally, on 2 July, they began their journey. The prospect of journeying over land and water in a huge, wheeled conveyance, holding five adults and five children, seems not to have been daunting; the travellers of the nineteenth

Above: Georgina Hogarth.

century were not so faint-hearted, perhaps, as their modern equivalents. They travelled along the dusty summer roads of France, with Dickens taking in every sight and sound with his quick and voracious perception.

They arrived at their destination two weeks later, tired and jaded by incessant movement. Dickens was at first appalled by the desolate grandeur of what was an Italian palace, in a district outside Genoa known as Albaro, but the family and servants soon filled it with their own particular energy. Dickens himself, daily expecting his usual desk and writing equipment which had not yet arrived from London, threw himself into learning Italian; such was his native intelligence, in fact, that within a short period he had a working understanding of the language.

He was both impressed and horrified by Genoa itself. He was haunted, in particular, by its fantastic decay; the very houses seemed like relics of some ancient time, while the great palaces of the sixteenth century were now mere shells in which various shops and stalls were erected. The odour of the slovenly lanes and streets was intense, while the statues and monuments of the town seem bleared with age and neglect. It was the first time he had encountered a Catholic culture, and he could not help but be startled by all the splendour and spectacle attendant upon the rites and practices of that Church; he was dismissive of the priests and monks, amused by the low whisperings of the services, but genuinely admiring of the decorative architecture of the churches themselves. And then beyond the city lay the sea like a dream, that 'would wash out everything else, and make a great blue blank of your intellect'.

Above: The harbour at Genoa.

He was being entertained by various local eminences, and entertaining them in turn in his usual dazzlingly amiable way. But there was one incident that reveals some part of his true character. He had been dining late in Genoa itself and, suddenly realizing that the gates of the city were closed at midnight, he felt obliged to rush out through the streets in a great hot haste to be gone – so hasty, in fact, that he fell across a pole and was badly bruised as he sprawled in the dust. He was terrified of being locked in, and in that fear it is possible to glimpse a reawakening of all the childhood anxieties that he experienced in the precincts of the Marshalsea prison. It cannot be a coincidence that, immediately after this incident, he again began to suffer those pains in the side that he had experienced when working in the blacking factory by the Thames. The slightest accident could provoke his primal fears.

After three months the Dickens entourage left its ancient house in Albaro and moved to the Palazzo Peschiere in Genoa itself. His writing equipment had by now safely arrived from London, and he was eager to begin work on a Christmas story to succeed *A Christmas Carol*. But he could not muster the rhythms of composition; he told Forster that he missed the streets of London, the 'magic lantern' of his imagination in which he saw wonderful scenes and images. The bells of Genoa surrounded him instead, and he railed against the noise.

But then, in some flash of recognition, their sound reminded him of the church bells of London; the story itself emerged in this act of imaginative homecoming. It was to be called *The Chimes*, and would deal with the endless miseries of the poor in the face of all the neglect and brutality that beset them on the streets of London. As soon as he could believe himself to be in London, he could begin to write. The weather all around him, however, was worse even than the weather of the great metropolis. 'Yesterday,' he wrote in one letter, 'in pure determination to get the better of it, I walked twelve miles in mountain rain.' This 'determination', this single-minded will 'to get the better' of any difficult or threatening situation, is pure Dickens. This state of mind was matched in any case by his general fury in the composition of *The Chimes*. 'My hair is very lank,' he wrote, 'my eyes have grown immensely large; and the head inside the hair is hot and giddy... I have undergone as much sorrow and agitation as if the thing were real.' To him, in fact, his imagination was reality itself.

Then the completed story had at once to be shown to others in order to affirm his own mastery. It had also to be shared by others so that his own feelings might be amplified by sympathy. So he decided to return to London, simply in order to read out his seasonal tale to a select group of friends. He told Forster that he would arrive on the first day of December, perhaps a rash prophecy in an age of uncertain and sometimes dangerous travelling; but he always prided himself upon his punctuality. He was never late for anything, not even the most insignificant meeting. He was in that sense obsessed with time, and that obsession has in turn been related to some psychological complexity in which fear and guilt are closely intertwined.

The same curious psychology can be found in a note to his wife while he was on the road to England. 'Keep things in their places,' he enjoined her. 'I can't bear to picture them otherwise.' He did not wish any furniture or household item to be moved from its familiar place. He wanted to be able to 'picture' his Italian residence with serene confidence in its stability. It is hard to resist the conclusion that this overwhelming desire sprang in part from his childhood memory of endless house moves; he must have recalled, too, the period when all the familiar household items were sold off to pay his father's

Above: Dickens reading The Chimes *to a select group of his friends, including Carlyle, Maclise and Forster.*

debts. That is why his fiction is filled with bright hearthsides, snug quarters and 'cosy' houses, where all threat of change or decay is held at bay.

The journey back to London was beset by foul weather and perilous crossings – he and his guide, Louis Roche, had to cross the Simplon Pass on foot in the small hours of the morning – but of course he arrived in London a day ahead of schedule. Then he immediately plunged into a hurricane of engagements and dinners. His friends duly gathered at the house of John Forster in Lincoln's Inn Fields for a private reading of *The Chimes*, which they greeted with manifold tears. Once more the image of the Victorians, stern and repressed in equal measure must be revised.

Dickens himself was pleased by the reception and wrote to his wife in exultant terms. 'You would have felt, as I did, what a thing it is to have power.' This notion of 'power' is central to any understanding of the novelist's genius; it is implicated in the whole range of nineteenth-century concerns, scientific, imperialistic, economic. He was truly a representative of his time because he was animated by its most vital principles.

Before returning to his family in Genoa, he visited Paris. He was in the company of the Shakespearean actor William Charles Macready, and through him met various Parisian notables. Among them were Victor Hugo and Alexandre Dumas, but in his correspondence Dickens registers no particular impression of their character. It is almost as if he did not care about meeting them, and took no great pains to form any closer acquaintance. The truth is that he did not particularly welcome the company of other eminent writers and was not greatly interested in their work; he always preferred the society of those less significant than himself. Dickens surrounded himself with journalists and actors because they represented no threat or challenge to his pre-eminence. Writers like Hugo or Dumas were not in quite the same category, and were therefore to be left alone.

He returned to family life in Genoa, but soon prepared for a longer journey throughout Italy in order to gather material for the new travel book he was contemplating. There was, however, one piece of unfinished business. He had encountered an Englishwoman, Augusta de la Rue, who lived in Genoa with her Swiss husband. Quickly becoming aware that she suffered from some kind of nervous disorder, Dickens offered his services as a healer. Several years earlier, he had become intensely interested in mesmerism, especially that form used by certain medical practitioners, and had discovered that he himself was an expert mesmerist who could send people into a 'magnetic sleep' with the movement of his hands across their heads and bodies. It is perhaps not surprising that a man of his abundant energy could control the energy of others.

So he sent Mrs de la Rue into a mesmeric slumber or trance, in which she revealed that she had constant hallucinations of a phantom threatening her. Dickens himself believed that the phantom was a 'representative' of a diseased nervous system, a remarkable intuition which he followed with a course of healing that seemed to have some salutary effect upon his 'patient'. But there was an unexpected problem. Catherine Dickens grew jealous of his constant attention to Mrs de La Rue, and protested to him. He was indignant at her suggestion of intimacy, but felt the need to placate her with endless reassurances. It was not a happy episode in his domestic history, and it anticipates greater marital disaster.

Yet husband and wife soon set off upon an extended tour of their temporarily adopted country. They travelled south to Pisa and to Rome, taking in the 'sights' (and smells) en route. In Rome itself Dickens explored the ruins

Opposite: The actor, William Charles Macready.
Above: Cartoon of Dickens in Paris.

of ancient time with a certain morbid relish, but he professed to find the rituals of the Catholic Church no more than a solemn pantomime. He likened the pope to a Guy Fawkes carried on the shoulders of the Swiss Guards like a ridiculous puppet. That strain of English sensibility was also evident in his appreciation of Italian art, about which he adopted a tone of robust common sense. He was by no means an aesthete or art historian, and his artistic judgements are no more than an inspired version of the 'I know what I like' school.

From Rome he and Catherine travelled down to Naples, where Dickens made a point of climbing Mount Vesuvius while it was in a state of eruption. He mounted higher and still higher, as the ash and smoke billowed around, until at last he was able to look into the mouth of the flaming crater. It was a

Above: Naples.

very dangerous exploit, but one that might have been expressly designed for a man of Dickens's temperament. 'We looked down into the flaming bowels of the mountain,' he wrote, 'and came back again, alight in half a dozen places, and burnt from head to foot.' Again, it is pure Dickens.

On his return to England, after a sojourn in Italy that had lasted for an entire year, the fury continued. He decided to act in, and stage-manage, *Every Man in His Humour* by Ben Jonson. He wanted to compose another Christmas story, to capitalize on the success of those he had already written. But, more importantly, he decided that the time was opportune for a new national daily newspaper – which he, of course, would organize and edit. His closest friends advised him against undertaking such a dangerous project; it would injure his real work as a writer and fatally divert his energies. And yet he was adamant. His early experience as a reporter convinced him that he was sufficiently well acquainted with the workings of the journalistic world. It was a period, too, of growing political unrest and economic disorder. The Corn Laws, in particular, were causing immense distress. These laws, which applied duties upon the

importation of foreign corn, had already exacerbated the effect of the 'potato famine' in Ireland, where thousands were dying every week, and had been the cause of riots in England. Anyone on the side of 'reform' in political and social affairs had found a rallying ground in the Anti-Corn Law League. The appearance of a radical and pro-reform national newspaper, then, might have an immense effect upon public opinion. Dickens could only rise to the challenge.

There was also another reason for his new-found enthusiasm for journalism. The poor sales of *Martin Chuzzlewit* had persuaded him that his popularity

Top: Dickens acting in Every Man in his Humour *at St James' Theatre, 1845.*
Above: Satirical comment on the repeal of the Corn Laws.

might not be a permanent phenomenon. 'And most of all,' he wrote to John Forster, 'I have, sometimes, that possibility of failing health or fading popularity before me, which beckons me to such a venture when it comes within my reach.' The fear, then, was of some possible breakdown in health or reputation. Even despite the manifold signs of his success, he was never free of anxiety. This fear was, of course, the spur to his achievement, but it also provoked him into strange actions and even stranger judgements.

There were others, however, who concurred with his plans. Two leading industrialists from the north of England offered financial support; they were

part of the 'railway interest', which the newspaper would eventually represent, and manifested a twin commitment to industrial progress and economic reform. Dickens was also joined in the venture by Joseph Paxton, the quondam gardener who had in true Victorian fashion worked his way from poverty into power and acclaim; his most notable achievement was perhaps the Crystal Palace, built for the Great Exhibition of 1851, and to his contemporaries he was a hero of the philosophy of 'self-help'.

Everything seemed set fair for success, therefore. Dickens hired a knowledgeable and experienced staff, who had various responsibilities in departments such as 'naval news', 'railway news' and 'clerical news'. Curiously, perhaps, he had decided to employ his father as head of the reporting staff; this might seem a strange appointment, given John Dickens's general reputation for fecklessness, but familial loyalty may have outweighed discretion. It was also, of course, a way of giving him a salary and therefore removing him as a financial dependent.

The first number of the *Daily News*, coming from the presses in a court off Fleet Street, appeared on Wednesday, 21 January 1845. It contained reports of the latest proceedings in Parliament, culminating in a speech by Robert Peel on the Corn Laws and an editorial urging their repeal. It also contained an

Above: A contemporary cartoon satirizes the pretensions of the press.

article by Dickens himself, in which he outlined the policy of the new paper. 'The principles advocated by *The Daily News*,' he wrote, 'will be Principles of Progress and Improvement, of Education, Civil and Religious, and Equal Legislation – Principles such as its Conductor believes the advancing spirit of the time requires, the Condition of the country demands, and Justice, Reason and Experience legitimately sanction.'

His emphasis upon 'the spirit of the time' was characteristic, since there has

never been an age so conscious of itself and of its destiny. The phrase 'Condition of the country' also invoked what was generally known as the 'Condition of England' question, which asked how the most powerful nation in the world could harbour so much poverty, ignorance and sickness. It purported to lead the world, and indeed owned a large share of it, but the circumstances of its cities were a standing reproach and infamy. To add a certain variety to the otherwise serious tone of the journal, Dickens had also begun printing his reflections on Italy under the title of 'Travelling Letters Written on the Road'.

The first issue was not altogether a success, with rumours that the printers had been drunk 'on the stone', but Dickens fully believed that the standard of news and reflective commentary would soon reach its proper level. Then a familiar pattern began to emerge in his own activity. He quarrelled with the proprietors of the newspaper. In particular he began to remonstrate with Mr Bradbury, who, like many proprietors, wished to be engaged in the daily admin- istration of his concern. Dickens had always demanded to be in sole charge of any business with which he was acquainted, and he interpreted Bradbury's behaviour as interference with, and insubordination of, his editorial privileges.

Above: Dickens speaking at the Dulwich College Charity Meeting at the Adelphi Theatre, London.

The truth is that he could never work with anyone who was even nominally his superior. He was too highly strung, too sensitive to slights or rebuffs, to be able

to accommodate himself to the general turbulence of business affairs. And so he simply walked away. After seventeen days in the office he resigned as editor. He would continue to contribute articles and essays, but his active involvement in the *Daily News* came to an abrupt halt.

It may not have been entirely coincidental, however, that he had already been visited by vague premonitions of another novel. He was once more consumed by restlessness and a general over-excitability that rendered him fiery and nervous. Catherine had just suffered the miseries of another pregnancy, but Dickens seems to have refused to sympathize with her condition. He described her as another 'Joanna Southcott', a prophetess who suffered from phantom pregnancy, and in that disparaging remark there is perhaps an indication of growing disaffection. He had decided without consultation, too, that he and his entire family should once more decamp to Europe, where he might live more cheaply and where he might be free of all the pressures and claims that he had experienced in England.

He chose Lausanne, a clean and prosperous Swiss town on the banks of Lake Geneva, as a suitable refuge for his embattled spirit. He liked Switzerland itself; the people were clean, neat and punctual in all their dealings. These were the virtues that Dickens most admired, in himself as well as in others. The family found a charming villa, covered with roses, on the side of the hill overlooking the lake. It was all sufficiently agreeable, but very soon Dickens was wandering in the Alpine regions where the extremes of his nature might be reflected in the wilder scenery. He was also affected by the spectacle of the

Above: All the news that's fit to print.

medieval castle Chillon, the ancient dungeons of which still exuded an atmosphere of torture and incarceration. He was always very sensitive to the *genius loci*.

The prison fortress gave Dickens an opportunity to revile the myth of 'the good old times'; he cordially detested any false nostalgia for earlier periods of human history, believing quite sensibly that they were crueller and more violent than was generally perceived. He was very much a nineteenth-century progressive in that sense; despite his imaginative sympathy for all the defeated and oppressed, his consciously articulated opinions were always on the side of nineteenth-century improvements.

He had left the *Daily News* partly to concentrate his energies upon a new novel, and within a very short time he had hit upon

its title. *Dombey and Son* was started in good spirits, and the early chapters were read to an admiring circle of new friends whom Dickens had acquired in Lausanne. The success of the reading, in fact, encouraged Dickens in the belief that he might give such public performances in a more professional way. It was the seed from which a great enterprise would one day spring.

But he was not able to work continuously or for very long. He was having similar problems with the fourth of his Christmas books, provisionally entitled *The Battle of Life*, and his slow progress threw Dickens into agonies of indecision. Should he give up *The Battle of Life*? Should he turn it into a full-scale novel? He blamed his incapacity, in part, upon the quietness of Lausanne itself. He experienced once more 'that craving for streets' which had pursued him in the past; London was still the magic lantern of his imagination.

Above: Dickens at his desk.

CHAPTER SIX

The great performer

The household left for Paris; but the capital did not impress Dickens on this trip. He found the Parisians, for example, nonchalant to the point of incivility. Yet on his return from Paris he was as dissatisfied as ever, with London in particular and with the world in general.

Too late to say, put the curb on, and don't rush at hills. I am the wrong man to say it to. I am incapable of rest. I am quite confident I should rust, break, and die, if I spared myself. Much better to die, doing.

Charles Dickens

It seems, in fact, that he was suffering from some more general instability or debility. Ever since his return from America he had been hardly able to settle to anything. He quarrelled with John Forster, his most intimate friend, and argued violently with the artist George Cruikshank on the subject of alcohol. Cruikshank was a reformed alcoholic who, like many converts, proceeded at once to the most violent extremes of temperance. In Dickens's company he even tried to dash a glass of wine out of a woman's hand, and the novelist turned upon him with ferocity. It was his settled belief that there was nothing wrong with wines or spirits in moderation; that, indeed, they added to the

Above: Paris.
Opposite: Mr Bumble from David Copperfield.

happiness of life. This was Dickens's philosophy in all matters of entertainment and indulgence. The working people, in particular, must be allowed to alleviate their hard lives by any moderate means at their disposal.

In the middle of all this restlessness and instability he decided to turn his attention to another series of amateur theatricals, in which once more friends and acquaintances were dragooned mercilessly into taking part. The popularity of the amateur stage is, in fact, one of the peculiarities of mid-nineteenth-century English culture. It may have represented some wish to escape from the conditions of society into a dream world, but it also marks the presence of some genuine communal spirit. For Dickens himself, of course, it meant that he could suspend the real world for a little while in favour of a bright parade of imaginative figures. He himself was also constantly moving – to Broadstairs, to Birmingham, to Scotland, to London. 'I am at a great loss for means of blowing my superfluous steam off,' he wrote, 'and find myself compelled to tear up and down…by express trains.' It is odd, perhaps, that the metaphor of steam should link him to the railway train's remorseless motion.

Some of that steam was expended in a large and complex charitable work which he undertook with Angela Burdett Coutts, a young woman of considerable inheritance, who believed that her wealth should be used for the improvement of the less fortunate. The plight of 'fallen women', for example, was then of considerable public concern. It is supposed that there were between seventy and ninety thousand prostitutes upon the streets of London, with all the attendant problems of sickness and degradation. Dickens

Above: Urania Cottage – the 'home for fallen women' founded by Dickens and Angela Burdett Coutts.

and Miss Burdett Coutts had determined to set up a 'Magdalen' or place of refuge for those women who wished to relinquish their unhappy trade, and eventually to return to some semblance of conventional life.

Dickens found a house, Urania Cottage, in Shepherds Bush which with his usual dispatch and energy he transformed into a 'home for fallen women'. He arranged the daily routine, chose the furniture and curtains, supervised the sanitary arrangements, set up a disciplinary code, and even determined the cut and cloth of the uniform that the young women were to wear. He wrote detailed letters of advice to the matron of the 'home' and often intervened personally in the running of the establishment. It was a thorough and compli-cated act of social philanthropy, fuelled also by his obsessive concern for the young women them-selves; he chose those he deemed most suitable, and followed up their activities with curiosity and

zeal. He recommended some for expulsion, and sent others off to Australia in order to begin a 'new life'. It is almost as if he were picking characters for a fictional experiment.

Yet there is a difference. In his fictional account of 'fallen women', such as Nancy in *Oliver Twist* or Emily in *David Copperfield*, an element of sentimentality or pathos soon intrudes. But in his relationships with the real women of Urania Cottage he was severely pragmatic and practical in his approach; he was a disciplinarian by temperament, and desired a well-ordered world. In his fiction, however, all such barriers and orders dissolve. His work is more capacious than his character.

Above: Angela Burdett Coutts.

Thus, in Dombey and Son, which he was writing in the same period that he was organizing Urania Cottage, he reflects upon the seeds of profligacy and vice that were sown in the poor tenements of London. 'Then should we stand appalled to know,' he wrote, 'that where we generate disease to strike our children down and entail itself on unborn generations, there also we breed,

by the same certain process, infancy that knows no innocence, youth without modesty or shame, maturity that is mature in nothing but in suffering and guilt, blasted old age that is a scandal on the form we bear.' In his imaginative life he suffered with the suffering; in his practical life he felt obliged to discipline them with codes and regulations. In the prison scenes of his novels he languished with the inmates and depicted with absolute candour the horrors of the incarcerated; in his public comments upon the prison system he repeatedly emphasized the need for hard and futile labour as the best antidote to crime. It is the difference between the waking mind of the responsible man and the imaginative gift of the child who still slept within him.

In many respects, of course, he still resembled a child in his spontaneity and high spirits. He was always very good with small children. He was an excellent father to his own infants, but grew steadily more impersonal with them as they grew into adult estate. On yet another tour of his amateur theatrical company, raising money for another 'good cause', it was remarked by one of the actors that 'there was a positive sparkle…of holiday sunshine about him; he seemed to radiate brightness and enjoyment'. He entered every occasion with an enormous fund of hilarity, so that even the most commonplace event could become exhausting for those caught up in the full

Above: One of Dickens's fictional prison scenes — Fagin in the condemned cell in Oliver Twist.

whirlwind of his gaiety. Even in relatively old age, when he was sick and ailing, he would mimic the routines of the clown in the pantomime. Those around him were clearly intimidated, as well as enlivened, by his manner. It is curious to report that there were others who, on being introduced to him, believed that they should act in a 'Dickensian' manner in his presence and become more outrageous or absurd than they really were. Such is the force of genius in the world.

There were occasions, too, when Dickens himself did not wish to leave the bright world of childhood enchantment that surrounded him. At the end of his amateur theatricals, for example, he lamented the return to the domestic hearth that he celebrated in his fiction. 'I am very miserable,' he wrote in his exaggeratedly jocose manner, which at least bore a hint of his true feelings. 'I loathe domestic hearths. I yearn to be a vagabond. Why can't I marry Mary?' Mary was a character in one of the farces that the troupe had just performed; but he might also have been invoking the spirit of Mary Hogarth.

It may seem strange that a public man so beset by the ills of the age, and so pronounced in his campaign against them, should still seek the safety of some fantasy world; but it is yet another aspect of Dickens's divided temperament. The death of his sister Fanny from the complications of tuberculosis only served to confirm his generally unsettled and unhappy state. By her deathbed his mind wandered over his earliest years, when they had been companions, and over that dream of childhood from which he had not yet fully awakened.

He found himself unable to write a novel, but from Fanny's death and from his own experience of sorrow emerged the 'Christmas book' for that season. It was entitled *The Haunted Man*, and work upon its composition was slow and fitful. A general pattern of writing may be said to manifest itself here: there was a blockage, when he felt the strangest miseries crowding around him, and then a sudden release of words that carried him forward. Like a child again, he could not help but relieve his feelings in a direct fashion. So the Haunted Man is in a sense Dickens, haunted by himself. 'No mother's self-denying love,' a character confesses in the course of the narrative, 'no father's counsel, aided me… My parents, at the best were of that sort whose care soon ends, and whose duty is soon done; who cast their offspring loose; early, as birds do theirs; and, if they do well, claim the merit; and if ill, the pity.' This flood of self-pity and regret was always waiting to overwhelm him.

I saw them in the fire but now. They come back to me in music, in the wind, in the dead stillness of the night, in the revolving years.

The Haunted Man, *Chapter One*

And then something else happened. An elderly gentleman, Sir Charles Dilke, was engaged in conversation with John Forster. Knowing that Forster was Dickens's intimate friend, the gentleman recalled an incident many years before when, with John Dickens, he had visited the young Charles who was then working in a blacking factory near the Strand. Half in pity and half in admiration, Dilke presented the boy with half a crown. In return the young

Charles Dickens gave him a very low bow. Forster was unwise enough to repeat this story to Dickens at their next encounter. On hearing it, Dickens was silent for several minutes. A secret had been revealed. His hidden past had come into the light.

He was so affected by the incident that, a few evenings later, he sat down at his desk and began to write the narrative of his early years. In this he concealed nothing, pouring out all the agony and longing of his nature in the defining account of his childhood. He wrote of the blacking factory and of his father's confinement in the Marshalsea; he wrote of his fears and of his resentments against his parents. It might all have happened yesterday. Indeed, for Dickens, it was even closer than that.

Then, by some strange alchemy, Dickens began to contemplate the outline of *David Copperfield*. He may have intended to write an autobiography, beginning with this anguished account of childhood, but the fictional narrative drew so directly from his private memories that all other schemes were at once set aside. Forster had already suggested to him that he write a novel in the first person, and of course with the progress of little David from misery to happiness he had found the perfect subject. He travelled to Yarmouth on the east coast, intuition guiding him to a bleak shoreline not unlike that of the Kentish Medway in his childhood, and here he walked twenty-three miles along the shore. Even then the shades of Peggotty, Barkis and Little Em'ly were calling to him.

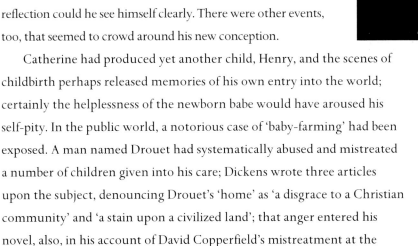

When Forster pointed out that David Copperfield boasted the same initials as Charles Dickens, only in reverse, he seemed astonished. He was superstitious about his 'fate', despite his sceptical pronouncements on occult matters, and he found in this coincidence a confirmation of his new venture. Indeed, the novel does represent a 'reverse' image of Dickens himself, as if only in reflection could he see himself clearly. There were other events, too, that seemed to crowd around his new conception.

Catherine had produced yet another child, Henry, and the scenes of childbirth perhaps released memories of his own entry into the world; certainly the helplessness of the newborn babe would have aroused his self-pity. In the public world, a notorious case of 'baby-farming' had been exposed. A man named Drouet had systematically abused and mistreated a number of children given into his care; Dickens wrote three articles upon the subject, denouncing Drouet's 'home' as 'a disgrace to a Christian community' and 'a stain upon a civilized land'; that anger entered his novel, also, in his account of David Copperfield's mistreatment at the hands of the Murdstones. Strangely enough, he also began suffering

Above: Henry and Francis Dickens.
Opposite: David Copperfield arrives at the home of his aunt, Betsy Trotwood.

those kidney pains that had afflicted him as a child in the blacking warehouse; to dwell upon past cares seems to have induced in him ancient ailments.

He moved restlessly from one part of the country to the next, even while in the throes of composition. Eventually he decided to settle on the Isle of Wight, and found a house in Bonchurch where the whole family might comfortably dwell; there was a waterfall in the garden which, with his usual ingenuity, he turned into a shower-bath. But nothing seemed to be able to arouse his spirits. He was feeling morose and restless, with what he called 'extreme depression of mind and a disposition to shed tears from morning to night'. He did not stop to consider whether the effect of unravelling his childhood in *David Copperfield* had played some part in this enervation; instead, he blamed it upon the climate of the island.

Another incident there galvanized him for a moment. A friend, the caricaturist John Leech, had been concussed by a great wave rolling down

upon him while he was bathing near the shore, and was then stricken by some kind of brain fever. Dickens's evident talents as a healer were now required, and he hypnotized Leech into a 'magnetic slumber' which effectively cured him. He joked that he might set himself up in business as a mesmeric doctor, and there is no doubt that he would have been a successful one.

Since the atmosphere of Bonchurch had proved to be injurious to his health and work, Dickens and his entourage moved on to Broadstairs and then, later, to Brighton. Yet of course he had to return in the end to London, that lodestone rock against which he had once been hurled but to which he had clung ever since. There would come a time when he would profess to despise the city, but he never left it. His dying words

Above: Uriah Heep.

formed a wish to return there. But now its crueller
realities kept on breaking through. He witnessed a
double execution in public: a Mr and Mrs Manning
were hanged outside the prison in Horsemonger Lane
for the murder of Mrs Manning's lover, and Dickens
could hardly resist the spectacle. He became part of the
crowd milling just beyond the rope and the trap-door,
and in two letters to *The Times* conjured up the images
of 'screeching and laughing... cries and howls' which
attended the ritual punishment. It had become his firm
belief that public hanging was a wicked and fruitless act
of vengeance, and that capital punishment, if it had to
be undertaken, should be enacted within the seclusion
and silence of the prison walls.

And, at last, *David Copperfield* was finished. Filled with memories of his own
childhood despair, and his own adult ambition, the novel represented his life
as seen in a convex mirror, in which the personages take on strange shapes
and stranger attitudes. It is populated by Uriah Heep, Mr Micawber, Mr Dick,
Mr Murdstone, Peggotty, Steerforth, Little Em'ly and Betsey Trotwood, all of
them immortalized by Dickens's longing for them to be real. Immediately
on completion of the novel he wrote to Forster, 'If I were to say half of what
Copperfield makes me feel tonight, how strangely, even to you, I should be
turned inside out! I seem to be sending some part of myself into the Shadowy
World.' Yet it is hard to say which, for Dickens, was the real world and which
the world of shadows. He had no doubt about the power and efficacy of the
book itself. 'Of all my books,' he said a few months before his death, 'I like
this the best.'

Even while continuing work upon it, however, he was busily engaged in
another literary venture. He was still preoccupied with the notion of starting a
weekly periodical or miscellany into which all the currents of his age might be

Above: Mr Micawber.

directed. A weekly periodical, too, would provide the opportunity for earning substantial sums of money. So he began work on his new design. His experiences with proprietors had not been happy, and with any new venture he wanted absolute power. It would not only be 'conducted' by Charles Dickens, but would also be owned by Charles Dickens.

The name he eventually chose was taken out of Shakespeare. Yet *Household Words* was to be a reflection of the mid-nineteenth century, 'this summer-dawn of time' as Dickens called it. When later commentators use 'Dickensian' as a mark of some opprobrious social evil, the novelist's own more optimistic note

must also be remembered. The periodical was to include poems, short stories, essays, articles and serial novels. It published work by the novelists Elizabeth Gaskell and Edward Bulwer Lytton, as well as accounts of the latest scientific invention or the most recent public scandal. And, of course, it also included articles by Dickens himself; he knew well enough that he was the principal 'draw' of the magazine.

He wrote pieces on ragged schools and cheap theatres, on homeless women and seaside resorts, on murderers and striking workers; he composed articles on the mad women who walked through the London streets, and the emaciated women who lingered at the doors of the workhouses demanding entrance. He was pre-eminently a London reporter, observing all the signs and tokens of the first metropolis that had ever emerged upon the face of the world. He also contributed more personal essays largely concerned with childhood, essays that rank in pathos and sympathy with any passages in his mature fiction.

Above: Engraving of a workroom in a ragged school.

'Where have you been all day?'

'About the streets.'

'What have you had to eat?'

'Nothing.'

'Come,' said I. 'Think a little. You are tired and have been asleep, and don't quite consider what you are saying to us. You have had something to eat today. Come! Think of it!'

'No, I haven't. Nothing but such bits as I could pick up about the market. Why, look at me!'

She bared her neck, and I covered it up again.

From 'A Nightly Scene in London', published in Household Words

But he was a working editor as much as a writing editor; he edited and 'marked up' thousands of pieces each year, taking extraordinary pains with even the slightest article so that it would maintain the consistently 'bright' tone of the periodical. He had hired an assistant, W.H. Wills, and even when he was noisily engaged in his seaside holidays, great packets of articles and correspondence would pass between him and the office in Wellington Street. He continued this work for the rest of his life. It would have been a full and arduous post for any ordinary person, but it was only one of Dickens's multifarious activities – including the not inconsiderable feat of writing some of the finest novels in the English language. He knew that he was remarkable and, in the early days of *Household Words*, he surprised even himself by laying down *David Copperfield* in order to write a graceful essay entitled 'A Child's Dream of a Star'. 'What an amazing man!' he said of himself.

He has been described as the greatest editor of his period and, indeed, with its mixture of social comment and engaging fiction, *Household Words*

Above: A young girl working as a street seller.

managed to attract and retain a very large number of readers. The initial circulation was one hundred thousand and in succeeding years, until his death, despite temporary dips in its fortunes, it never really declined in popularity. Its influence was immense, also, with Dickens's forays into the evils associated with bad sanitation and bad housing materially assisting the cause of mid-nineteenth-century reform.

He was also active in more particular causes. With the novelist Edward Bulwer Lytton he decided to establish a Guild of Literature and Art which would provide support for writers and artists whose careers had faltered. Dickens, perhaps more than any other writer of his time, was keen to uphold the 'dignity' of his profession; it was a measure of his own pride but also a reflection of his own anxieties about his future.

So with characteristic expedition he set to work on another round of amateur theatricals in order to finance the altruistic enterprise. He stage-managed and performed in a light comedy by Bulwer Lytton entitled *Not So Bad As We Seem*; he designed the set and helped to install it. Given the importance of the putative Guild, which he believed would entirely change the profession of authorship, he wished for a suitably grand audience. The Queen was invited; she accepted. He wrote to the Duke of Devonshire, asking if Devonshire House in Piccadilly might be used as a theatre for the occasion; the duke willingly agreed. All the commonplaces about Victorian 'stuffiness' seem, on closer examination, to dissolve. 'I beg you to let me see you before long,' the duke wrote, 'not merely to converse upon this subject, but because I have long had the greatest wish to improve our acquaintance.' So a duke addresses the son of an imprisoned bankrupt.

The drama was, as usual, conducted magnificently if magisterially by Dickens. He seemed incapable of failure at any task to which he set himself. A carpenter watching him from the wings remarked 'Ah, sir, it's a universal observation in the

Above: A front page of Household Words.

profession, sir, that it was a great loss to the public when you took to writing books!' He was speaking on behalf of the theatrical profession, of course, and Dickens accepted the tribute as a compliment.

His own acting was indeed of a high standard, although some believed that there was an edge of 'hardness' in his brilliancy of impersonation; it was as if he were forcing himself to excel. In one farce, performed as a kind of dramatic encore to the main play, he took no fewer than six parts without the audience realizing. He was also adept at comic improvisation and spontaneous repartee; but then it would be odd if the greatest comic writer of his generation did not possess such inimitable gifts.

The performances in London were succeeded by a grand provincial tour to cities such as Manchester, Birmingham and Liverpool. The last of these, according to Dickens, was 'blinded by excitement, gas, and waving hats and handkerchiefs'. He was exultant. 'I have been so happy in all this,' he wrote, 'that I could have cried.' If this seems to represent the laughter and tears of an over-excited child, then it is testimony to the over-whelming power of Dickens's feelings. He loved to hold an audience spellbound; he loved the gaslight and the melodrama; he loved, in other words, to be taken out of ordinary reality into some bright and coherent world of the imagination.

After their labours were completed, the cast would dine together each evening and then engage in general if rumbustious fun. They would play leapfrog, for example, and the spectacle of these distinguished Victorian men and women leaping and falling over one another provides another picture of nineteenth-century England. Certainly the glorious progress of the troupe instilled in Dickens some intimation of his own later role as a public entertainer, when he would cross the country giving public readings of his work to equally enthusiastic audiences. He remained an actor to the end.

Above: Dickens stage managing a production.

CHAPTER SEVEN

The burden of the world

As always happened, Dickens was pursued by low spirits at the close of his adventures in amateur dramatics. He suffered 'the melancholy of having turned a leaf in my life. It was so sad to see the curtain dropped...that something of the shadow of the great curtain which falls on everything seemed...to be upon my spirits.' It was his odd, old feeling of transience and decay, when the whole burden of the world seemed heavier after being momentarily lifted.

He was still pursued by the cares of that world. Dora, his infant daughter, became seriously ill with some kind of brain disease. Catherine Dickens was suffering from increasingly severe nervous disabilities, and was obliged to leave London for the gentler climate of Malvern. And then his father died. John Dickens had been suffering from complications of the urinary tract, and had been compelled to undergo a surgical operation without the benefit of anaesthetic. His room had become, in his son's redolent phrase, 'a slaughterhouse of blood'. His death came soon after these sanguinary proceedings and, in the immediate aftermath, Dickens forgot all the old fecklessness and chicanery for which he had often berated him. He would refer to him as 'my poor father', as if in death all wounds had been healed. He forgave him everything because now, for the first time, he saw him whole and entire. He realized, too, that without such a father there could never have been such a son.

In April 1851, he was addressing the General Theatrical Fund in a speech in which he paid tribute to the capacity of actors to take their place upon the stage even if they came from scenes of domestic suffering and even from death itself. Afterwards he was taken to one side by Forster, who informed him that little Dora was dead. He hurried back home and sat at the child's bedside all through the night. Only later did he break down in all the agonies of grief. He tried to quiet himself by undertaking a series of night walks through the city, where by the strange longings of his nature he found himself visiting, or revisiting, the darker recesses of London — the prisons, the asylums, the workhouses and the hospitals. He could only find

Top: The Thames at Westminster by Francis Moltino.
Above: St John's Gate, Clerkenwell.

relief, or release, in comprehending the greater sufferings of the urban world. It was as if he might merge with the stone and himself become stone.

Catherine, after returning to the scene of her infant's death, had to get away in order to preserve her precarious health. Dickens arranged for the family to decamp once more to Broadstairs. In addition, he decided that the house in Devonshire Terrace must be given up. He was always struck by the notion, albeit in a somewhat whimsical manner, that houses possessed personalities of their own; in this case, it had taken on a mournful one. There was a period of erratic

house-hunting until eventually he settled upon a good-sized property, Tavistock House, in Tavistock Square. In London guide-books that square would be consigned to Bloomsbury but, in fact, like the previous house in Devonshire Terrace, it is also close to Dickens's childhood haunts of Camden Town and Somers Town. It is noticeable, among born or adopted Londoners, that they rarely stray beyond their 'native' area; Dickens was no exception, and all his residences up to this date were within a short walking distance of each other.

The new house itself was in a shabby condition, and he laid out meticulous plans for its redesign and redecoration. He retreated to Broadstairs while the workmen were on the premises, although he could not resist coming back to see the signs (if any) of building progress. 'NO WORKMEN ON THE PREMISES!' Throughout the whole period of renovation he was thrown into comic agonies of despair and anger at the slow speed of the workmen, and of their general lack of interest in the proceedings. It is perhaps no coincidence that the novel then revolving in his mind would bear the title *Bleak House*. But eventually all was complete, just as Dickens had planned and foreseen it. Even the false book-backs in his library met his specifications, with titles like *The Virtues of Our Ancestors* – a very slim volume – and *Socrates on Wedlock*. It is well known that Socrates had a most shrewish wife.

Above: Fleet Street, London.
Opposite: Tavistock House, Tavistock Square, London.

Dickens had his own opinions on the subject of marriage, too, and in this period Catherine Dickens gave birth to another child. It might seem hard to subject her to yet another pregnancy, when her nervous and physical conditions were so obviously unbalanced by the experience. But he seemed not to consider her feelings on the matter. He simply concurred in the Victorian belief that it was just and proper to produce large families. In that sense he was conventional enough.

The question of his sexuality also arises here. He was not in conversation a prim or censorious man. He once declared that if a son of his was chaste, he would believe that there was something the matter with him. The steady fecundity of his wife would also suggest that he himself had a strong sexual appetite. Yet sex never enters his novels except in the most oblique fashion. This was partly a matter of public taste and expectation, but it is also intimately related to his childhood wanderings through London; in his essays, it becomes clear through hint and indirection that he witnessed the depravity of the streets and that he associated it with dirt and disgrace. It became part of his experience of 'blacking' and the blacking factory which threatened his cleanliness in every sense. So he was ambivalent upon the subject, driven to it by compulsion but fleeing it out of compunction.

He had also now reached the age of forty which, in his period, was the very threshold of middle age. Contemporaries were dying around him – 'what a field of battle' he complained – and there came upon him a suspicion that his old elastic energy was in shorter supply than in previous years. He complained that the 'spring' did not fly back with its usual celerity. And yet these are the remarks of an always over-active man.

He was deeply engaged, for example, upon the composition of *Bleak House* in monthly instalments. His early work upon the novel had been beset by his usual fits of 'violent restlessness'; he prowled around the edges of his story, but could not settle upon it. He said that it was like being 'driven away', with the sense that he did not wish to come too close to the springs or

Opposite: Dickens in middle age.

sources of his imagination. Yet as soon as he had embarked upon the tide of the narrative, it carried him along easily enough.

He was not engaged solely upon the novel. He was still conducting a weekly newspaper. He was assisting Miss Burdett Coutts in a project for building cheap housing for the working classes in Bethnal Green; he drew up

plans, also, for a library, a school and a savings bank to be erected on the same site. He was also dictating to his sister-in-law, Georgina, a history of England. He had originally composed it for the sake of his children, but realized that it might have a more general impact. In this narrative he describes the more colourful and adventurous aspects of English history, with a marked tendency to moralize upon the subject; he turned it into a drama, in other words, in which the principal character was social and intellectual progress.

His amanuensis, Georgina Hogarth, had now become indispensable to him and to his household. She acted as both nurse and companion to the children; she cared for her sister, too, during Catherine's frequent spells of illness. With Catherine unable or unwilling to take on the role of hostess, Georgina also acted in an unofficial capacity as 'lady of the house' when friends or visitors called.

That is why she accompanied the family when they decamped to Boulogne for the summer of 1853. Dickens had rented a large villa on the outskirts of the French town, where he worked upon *Bleak House* in the midst of long visits from various friends and acquaintances. It marked the beginning of an affection for France that was to endure for the rest of his life; he had even become reconciled to Paris. He grew a moustache and started to dress in the French fashion. He enjoyed his distance from England, even as in *Bleak House* he was composing a wholesale indictment of that country's society.

Above: Frontispiece for 1853 edition of Bleak House*.*

In this novel his native land was a place of fog and miasma, where the victims of the new urban world were heaped up in their thousands as if they were already dead. The judicial system was corrupt, but its labyrinthine network of chicanery and stale custom was a metaphor for the general state of the nation. The image of disease is also deeply impressed upon the narrative, where the stench of filth and the taint of decay creep from the lowest quarters of the poor – known in this novel as 'Tom-all-Alone's' or 'Tom' – to the highest reaches of the rich and the powerful. When Krook explodes by the strange process of spontaneous combustion, he only heralds the imminent fate of England itself.

> *Even the winds are his [Tom-all-Alone's] messengers, and they serve him in these hours of darkness. There is not a drop of Tom's corrupted blood but propagates infection and contagion somewhere...There is not an atom of Tom's lime, not a cubic inch of any pestilential gas in which he lives, not one obscenity or degradation about him, not an ignorance, not a wickedness, not a brutality of his committing, but shall work its retribution, through every order of society, up to the proudest of the proud, and to the highest of the high.*
>
> Bleak House, *Chapter XLVI*

The concerted labour upon *Bleak House* had exhausted Dickens; more than any previous novel it had depended upon a skilful and subtle interweaving of parts, in which comedy and pathos spring out of one another as naturally and as effortlessly as if the book were a living thing. The effect is perhaps the natural simulacrum of an urban culture in which happiness and sorrow, riches and poverty, avarice and famine existed beside each other. It is a novel filled with drama and with energy, with the great natural movement of crowds, and the symbolic power of the human spirit when viewed *in extremis*. It is, in every sense, a novel about London.

But in his restless state, he once more devised plans to travel onward.
He had decided upon a journey from France into Italy, but in the company
of friends rather than of family. He enlisted two acquaintances, the painter
Augustus Egg and the writer Wilkie Collins, on a two-month grand tour.
The choice of travelling companions was in no sense surprising. Both men
were younger than Dickens, and of a much freer temperament than such
contemporaries as Forster. Dickens had not the slightest intention of growing
old, and revelled in the company of those who could still boast something of

youth. His distaste for English life, as
evinced in *Bleak House*, also bred in him
a dissatisfaction with those who had
settled down into 'society' in their
middle age. He still called himself the
'Sparkler', or 'Albion's Sparkler',
but he could really only sparkle in the
presence of a sympathetic audience.

So he travelled through Italy and
Switzerland in high spirits. Egg and
Collins decided to grow moustache and

beard in imitation of Dickens, but the tuft on their faces was an abject failure.
Dickens was highly amused, although no doubt he sensed the pathos of those
who so quickly fell under his influence. He travelled back to Lausanne and to
Genoa – out of sheer nostalgia for his own presence there rather than for any
more ostensibly cultural reason – where he met old friends. Christiana Weller,
the young woman with whom he had once been much infatuated, was living
with her English husband in the Italian port. They had decided to set up their
household there under the direct impress of Dickens's previous example,
another instance of people trying to be more 'Dickensian' than Dickens
himself. His infatuation had passed, however, and he looked upon Christiana
with a cold eye; in a letter to Catherine, he surmised that 'household affairs

Above: Mr Chadband 'improving' a tough subject in Bleak House.

went a little to the wall'. In fact all his letters to England manifest a somewhat cruel objectivity concerning those around him; it was part of the 'hardness' in his nature that others observed, but there was always a sense in which Dickens was apart from other people. In some respects he was still the small child watching the world from a distance, as if it were all part of some adult game in which he refused to join.

On Dickens's return to England the railway authorities kept a train waiting upon his arrival, much to the annoyance of his fellow passengers. At this later date, however, it is sufficient proof of his fame. Such was his popularity, in fact, that he had been asked to give public readings of his Christmas books in Birmingham for the sake of the working men's institute there. He read twice from *A Christmas Carol*, once to an audience of working people who were allowed to purchase tickets at a specially reduced rate, and the success was overwhelming. Their laughter and applause 'animated me to that extent that I felt as if we were all bodily going up into the clouds together', and the furore encouraged him to consider more readings of a similar nature. He had experienced 'power' again, to employ his word, and he wanted more of the same.

He had been publishing a short episode of *A Child's History of England* in each weekly number of *Household Words*, but that spirited if histrionic document was not enough to hold the attention of readers. His publishers, Bradbury and Evans, and his friends urged him to begin a new novel within its pages; he saw the necessity for it, too, and immediately began to make plans for a new weekly story. What he looked for, he found. A theme 'laid hold of me by the throat', intimating that violence with which Dickens always described his activities. It was to be his

Top: William Wilkie Collins.
Above: The Bleak House Museum at Broadstairs.

first direct assault upon industrial capitalism, borne out of his observations of Manchester, Birmingham and elsewhere. It was to be written in an age when the words 'system' and 'statistic' became part of the general currency. It was to be called *Hard Times*. He travelled to Preston in order to describe a strike by weavers for *Household Words*. The trip also allowed him to observe the relations between workers and employers at first hand.

Yet his larger theme is concerned with the absence of fancy, and of wonder, in a world cajoled by a materialist and financial ethic. 'Now, what I want is, Facts.' The words of the schoolmaster Thomas Gradgrind open the book and, indeed, become an apt epigraph for its story of heartlessness and unimaginative greed. Dickens began in a rush, but the difficulty of keeping the story within the confines of short instalments proved to be 'CRUSHING'. Yet the device of a weekly narrative, first employed by him in *Master Humphrey's Clock* with *The Old Curiosity Shop*, proved successful. The sales of the periodical steadily rose, until they reached five or six times their previous level. He worked carefully, dividing the story in parsimonious fashion, and was inspired to use a language as plain and as compressed as anything he had ever written.

'I want to hear of you, mother; not of myself.'

'You want to hear of me, my dear? That's something new, I am sure; when anybody wants to hear of me. Not at all well, Louisa. Very faint and giddy.'

'Are you in pain, dear mother?'

'I think there's a pain somewhere in the room,' said Mrs Gradgrind, 'but I couldn't positively say that I have got it.'

Hard Times, *Chapter IX*

He decided to spend another summer in Boulogne, even as he continued his writing, and after the familiar delays in starting work, he became furiously re-engaged in the ongoing narrative. He had time and opportunity, however, to notice the military activity all around him. The Crimean War had begun just a month before his arrival in France. The shadow of that conflict was soon to cast a darker hue across his fiction, but even in its early stages he knew that it would be a giant distraction from the cause of social reform. The politicians would play the card of the patriot, and everything would be subsumed by a mighty war effort. All efforts for sanitary legislation, or for improved employment law, would now come to nothing.

It has been suggested that Dickens's novels did more for radical reform than the combined works of Marx and Engels. There is a limited truth to this. There is no doubt that his fiction awakened interest and concern in the plight of the poor, but his solutions to political problems were fatally implicated in the melodrama of his plots. He was a very practical man who helped thousands of people on a pragmatic basis, but he had no theoretical or (to use the contemporaneous word) systematic understanding of economic and political life.

It has already been observed how the latent memories of childhood fuelled his anger at specific abuses of children, and how the recollection of his own father's imprisonment seems to have fostered his abiding preoccupation with prisons and asylums. Where there was no imaginative bond or association, however, his interest in other social matters was more disciplined and objective. He was a reformer from principle, but he was no liberal by instinct.

After once hearing a young woman swear loudly in the street, he marched her to a police station and demanded that she be taken into custody. Even though he decried the necessity for capital punishment, he demanded hard and comfortless labour for prisoners; they should not be treated like 'pets', he argued, but instead their suffering should be exemplary. He was scathing about the 'savages' of North America and India, especially when they became popular tourist attractions in the exhibition halls of London. The list

Above: Dickens giving a public reading.

of examples could be multiplied indefinitely, but it is enough to say that in the general affairs of the day he was a disciplinarian as well as a reformer. He was a paternalist in all of his social dealings except when the fire of his thwarted past burned brightly in his imaginative works. In many respects, too, he was a conventional or old-fashioned patriot. A few weeks after his arrival in France he was putting candles in the window of his rented villa to celebrate the visit of Prince Albert to review the troops, and he was also becoming highly vociferous against the Russian enemy.

He had completed *Hard Times* in less than six months, and the strain of composing the weekly series had exhausted him. He travelled to London from Boulogne and engaged in a few days of 'dissipation' to expunge the memory of his recent labours. He was accompanied by Wilkie Collins in these revels, which probably amounted to little more than a ceaseless round of visits to the

Above: The inland view from the harbour at Boulogne, France.

theatres and restaurants of the city with (in his case) a few sips of gin and water in the gentlemen's clubs. When he returned to Boulogne he slept among the hills and fields, gradually turning brown in the rays of the sun.

But the 'great top' of *Household Words*, as he called it, still needed to turn. A new serial fiction by Mrs Gaskell seemed to have been growing wearisome both to Dickens and to the readers of the periodical; he could not cancel it at this late stage, and Mrs Gaskell refused to countenance any alterations in the weekly numbers. So he complained about her from a distance, and watched the lowered sales with chagrin. From Boulogne he sent packets of edited articles back to W. H. Wills in London, with repeated injunctions to 'brighten' the periodical at every opportunity. There is nothing he loathed more than dullness. For him it was like death itself. That was why, in the world, he seemed to be such a restless and impatient man.

On his return to London he immediately took the offensive against the established authorities. There was a great outbreak of cholera in the country, which had killed some twenty thousand people, and in *Household Words* Dickens raged against the unconcern and inefficiency of Parliament. The politicians were guilty of murder, he declared, and he came close to recommending a popular revolution to secure better conditions. The citizens of the country possessed 'a right to every means of life and health that Providence has provided for' and should now begin vociferously to demand it. Some of his more respectable friends questioned his sentiments, but he withdrew none of them. He seethed. He was, as he used to say, 'desperately in earnest'.

But his rage was also part of a larger distemper. His exhaustion after *Hard Times* could only be cured by further and yet further effort. He wanted to get away once more in order to start work upon a new

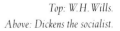

Top: W. H. Wills.
Above: Dickens the socialist.

novel. 'Restlessness, you will say,' he wrote to Forster. 'Whatever it is, it is always driving me, and I cannot help it.' He said that he had not worked for some nine or ten weeks. He had of course been steadily employed on *Household Words* and on composing his public pronouncements, and in fact had probably completed as much as any normal man would have achieved in the same period. But he had not started writing fiction again, and he chafed against his creative idleness. 'If I couldn't walk fast and far,' he said, 'I should just explode and perish.'

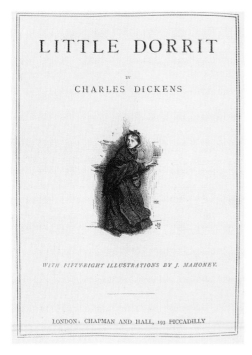

And then an envelope arrived upon his desk. He half-recognized the handwriting and put it to one side. When eventually he opened it, he discovered a letter from Maria Beadnell. Maria had been the young lady with whom he had fallen intensely and obsessively in love almost twenty-five years before. All at once he recalled everything from that time. He even remembered the colour and cut of the dresses which Maria used to wear. He sent her an impassioned letter in which he almost proposed to her for a second time. 'I have never been so good a man since, as I was when you made me wretchedly happy,' he told her. 'I shall never be half so good a fellow any more.' They had been 'the most innocent, the most ardent, and the most disinterested days of my life' when Maria Beadnell had been 'their Sun'. He rather coyly referred to Dora Spenlow in *David Copperfield* as a partial reflection of his youthful love. It did not seem to occur to him that Maria must have changed as he had changed, that twenty-five years forward she was not the pretty little charmer of those early London years. This was still his vision and, as always, his vision must correspond with reality.

And then he met her. She was plump, inclined to giggles and somewhat flirtatious. The vision departed. He was horrified by her and cut short their interview. She wrote to him again on several occasions, suggesting further

Above: The title page of Little Dorrit.

meetings, but he always declined. His excuse was that the demands of his art did not allow him to find time for her company. This was nonsense, of course, but he was desperate to avoid her. He then projected his feelings for her in the silly and garrulous figure of Flora Finching in *Little Dorrit*. When Maria Beadnell encountered this character, as surely she must have done, it would have come as a most heavy and bitter surprise.

> *'You mustn't think of going yet,' said Flora — Arthur had looked at his hat, being in a ludicrous dismay, and not knowing what to do: 'you could never be so unkind as to think of going, Arthur — I mean, Mr Arthur — or I suppose Mr Clennam would be far more proper — but I am sure I don't know what I'm saying — without a word about the dear old days gone for ever, however, when I come to think of it I dare say it would be much better not to speak of them and it's highly probable that you have some much more agreeable engagement and pray let Me be the last person in the world to interfere with it though there was a time, but I am running into nonsense again.'*

Little Dorrit, *Chapter XIII*

We learn something of Dickens's temperament, too, in the course of this little episode. He still held his most youthful yearnings close to him; he had never deserted his early years either in memory or in imagination. His vision was so intense that it took no account of any possible reality beyond its own bright range. And, when reality broke in, he had to reformulate it in terms of his art. It did not matter that Maria Beadnell would weep over her portrayal as Flora Finching; he could not help but put it down on paper. That was the only way in which his feelings could become real to himself. That was the only way in which he knew or understood himself. Other people were of slight consequence in the process of divining his own nature.

CHAPTER EIGHT

Home truths

Dickens had been unsettled by the strange meeting with Maria Beadnell, and to exorcize his unhappiness he plunged once more into public affairs. The prosecution of the Crimean War was being bogged down in delay and incompetence; out of an army of fifty-four thousand men, some forty thousand died from wounds or from the afflictions of malaria and typhus. The soldiers were being sent into battle without the proper equipment, and the hospitals at the 'front' were woefully insanitary.

So Dickens became a central figure in a newly formed organization, the Administrative Reform Association, which worked eagerly and vociferously for a wholesale reform of the parliamentary system. Dickens had always despised and distrusted Parliament, ever since the years he had spent as a reporter there, but the present state of the country was now 'like the general mind of France before the breaking out of the first Revolution', with a sullen workforce and an ignorant aristocracy. He feared that the wrath of the people

Above: The Crimean War.
Opposite: Flora's tour of inspection in Little Dorrit.

governed would utterly destroy the people governing. It was in this period, too, that he threw himself into the dramatic role of a lighthouse-keeper in Wilkie Collins's *The Lighthouse* so that he might be said literally to act out his own concerns as the ship of state headed for the rocks.

There was, however, one haven in his own life. In much earlier years, when he was a small boy, he and his father had roamed around the neighbourhood of Rochester in Kent; on one of these peregrinations John Dickens had pointed out to him a comfortable mansion that overlooked the Medway valley. He told his son that, if he worked hard enough, he might own such a house when he grew to be a man. It was called Gad's Hill Place. In the summer of 1855, by one of those curious coincidences that haunt Dickens's life (although he of all men knew that there was no such thing as

Above: Gad's Hill Place, Kent.

coincidence), that same house was put up for sale by one of his contributors to *Household Words*; he purchased it almost at once. It is another instance of the attractive power of his childhood; half of his decisions seem to have been determined by it. In this house, too, he would eventually die.

One of the first visitors to the new residence was the Danish writer Hans Christian Andersen; it would seem likely that the author of 'The Ugly Duckling' and 'The Little Mermaid' would be a settled favourite of Dickens, but the evidence suggests otherwise. Andersen was a difficult guest; his English was to all practical purposes unintelligible, and he had a habit of breaking down in tears. He was of a somewhat fey disposition, and would delight in picking nosegays in the woods around Gad's Hill in order to present them to his hosts; he was also an expert in cutting pretty shapes out of paper. Dickens was in many respects a conventional Englishman, and found Andersen's sensitive habits intensely annoying; after he had left he put a notice in the guest bedroom: 'Hans Christian Andersen slept in this room for five weeks which seemed to the family ages.' His daughters Mamey and Katey dismissed him as a 'bony bore'.

There was one incident, attendant upon this protracted visit, that reveals something of Dickens's own temperament. Andersen had been lamenting the bad reviews for one of his stories; he had in fact been crying on the lawn of Gad's Hill Place. Dickens drew a line in the dirt with his foot. 'That is criticism,' he told his guest. Then he wiped the line out with his foot. 'Thus it is gone.' Dickens rarely responded to criticism of his own work, except to amend mistaken matters of fact, but it was really only a sign of his sensitive temperament that he pretended to ignore the newspaper reviewers. He was in any case wise to ignore their strictures. He had already been written off as an 'extinct volcano', a writer whose best work lay in the past, and his latest work

Top: Mamey (Mary) Dickens.
Above: Hans Christian Andersen.

was dismissed as 'twaddle' or worse. His friends kept such criticism from him, as far as possible, so that he might work unimpaired and unimpeded.

When he was in the heat of composition, however, he knew his power well enough. He had already begun *Little Dorrit*, which had been provisionally entitled 'Nobody's Fault' as a satire upon indifferent officialdom and upon the labyrinthine convolutions of 'red tape' which hindered every political and social initiative. He decamped to Folkestone with his family and then, in an agony of restlessness, decided to travel on to Paris. It is interesting that at this stage in his career he seemed genuinely to dislike London. Did it remind him of his own old self? Or did it simply represent in monumental form the society that he had come to despise? Whatever the cause or explanation, he simply had to get away.

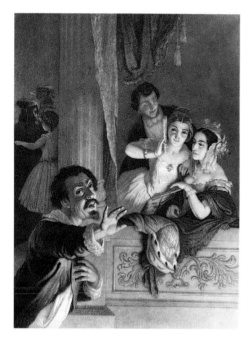

He had become much better known in Paris in any case, with a uniform edition of his books published by Hachette and daily instalments of *Martin Chuzzlewit* in one of the newspapers. He met all the 'lions' of the city, among them writers and bankers and statesmen, with whom he was soon on cordial terms. He spoke French fluently, having previously hired a tutor in that language, and at least on one level took pleasure in a place that depended upon *clarté* and *gloire* for its effects. Paris was truly the city of the spectacle, and its endless dramatic life had come to appeal to the theatrical aspects of Dickens's own character. He described its dramas and its dinners as if he were a stranger in a fairy-tale – one dinner table boasted 'oriental flowers in vases of golden cobweb' – but, curiously enough, he was once again less than enthusiastic about the native writers. He compared the celebrated novelist George Sands to 'the Queen's monthly nurse' who had 'nothing of the bluestocking about her, except a little final way of settling all your opinions with hers'.

Above: The dramatic life and theatres of Paris held great appeal for Dickens.

Yet he was well aware of failings closer to home. He visited the international art exhibition in Paris, and was unimpressed by the contribution of English artists. 'There is a horrid respectability about most of the best of them,' he wrote, 'a little, finite, systematic routine in them, strangely expressive to me of the state of England herself.' He saw images of the country's inanition and incompetence everywhere. Strangely enough, he found it even within his own fiction. He knew well enough that he could never present an authentically modern hero, complete with sexual passion, because the public morality of England would not countenance it. No character in an English novel could be provided with 'I will not say any of the indecencies you like, but not even any of the experiences, trials, perplexities, and confusions inseparable from the making or unmaking of all men!'

Above: Paris.

He seems here to be lamenting the absence of realism, at least in the image of French novels, and it throws a curious light upon his understanding and appreciation of his own work. Did he feel that there were vital elements necessarily missing from it? It may in part account for his assaults upon English society itself, as if it were effectively preventing him from fully exercising his own genius. Such reflections may only have been the fruit of tiredness or melancholy, however. He was hard at work upon *Little Dorrit*, which in its first few monthly numbers had acquired the largest readership Dickens had ever known. There was, surely, some consolation or reassurance in that.

But there is no doubt that he had grown tired of his conventional life. In Paris he had wandered through the theatres and dance halls, noting the places where the prostitutes gathered; whether or not he employed their services is an open question. On his return to England he found the Hogarths, his 'in-laws', to be a detestable presence in Tavistock House. But his complaints about their untidiness and dirtiness were essentially a displacement for more profound restlessness and unease in the company of his wife. He had grown tired of her. He did not want to grow old with her. 'I find that the skeleton in my domestic closet,' he wrote, 'is becoming a pretty big one.'

It is perhaps not surprising that he felt the need to act out his unhappiness. In the nineteenth century, amateur theatricals seemed to play a therapeutic as well as a cultural role. With Wilkie Collins he devised and produced what was called an 'arctic melodrama'. *The Frozen Deep* was staged in Tavistock House, and Dickens played the part of Richard Wardour, an explorer who had ventured into the wilderness in order to assuage or heal all the pains of a broken heart; he dies in the arms of the woman who had previously rejected him. It was all very stirring, and in fact Dickens's distraught performance reduced both cast and audience to real tears. Such was the force of his own performance, mingling loneliness with sorrow, that it pierced even those acting with him. It is a testimony to the power of his character, assumed or otherwise, and to the strength of his generally concealed feelings. At times of depression he always

Above: Dickens.

mourned the absence of one person, or companion, whom he had missed in life; his role as Richard Wardour brought those miseries to the surface.

The death of a close friend, Douglas Jerrold, provided him with an opportunity for reviving the play a few months after its first performances. All the proceeds would be placed in the purse of the widow. His ardour in the role of Wardour had not abated, and, indeed, Wilkie Collins reported that Dickens had 'electrified the audience'. The sense of energy here is almost literally conveyed; it was an age that discovered the ubiquity of electro-magnetic forces, after all, and some of the leading Victorians seem to have shared their power.

It is interesting in this context to consider his relationship with Queen Victoria herself. She was arguably the most important person in the world, but Dickens seems to have had a comparable sense of his own worth. Victoria had requested that *The Frozen Deep* be performed at Buckingham Palace, but Dickens refused on the grounds that he did not wish his daughters to be introduced at court in the role of amateur actresses. The Queen relented, and agreed to attend a performance of the play in a London hall known as the Gallery of Illustration. She enjoyed the occasion and, after the performance of the farce that followed the play, she requested that Dickens be presented to her. Dickens refused, believing that his dignity would be impaired if he came before her dressed in the costume of the farce; she asked again, and again he declined. It is a suggestive episode, demonstrating that Dickens's will was stronger than that of even his most powerful contemporaries. His often self-congratulatory stance was in that sense warranted by events. In a letter written at this time he referred to himself as 'the undersigned honeypot'.

The play had been such a success that there were repeated requests for its performance all over the country. It was decided, for example, that it should

Above: Dickens's daughters and Georgina Hogarth entertain Tennyson.

be staged in the Free Trade Hall in Manchester. The hall itself was too large for a cast of amateurs, and so Dickens searched for professional players. An acting family were recommended and soon hired. Mrs Ternan, together with her two daughters Maria and Ellen, travelled up to Manchester to assume their roles. It would not be too much to say that their arrival changed the entire course of Dickens's life. Maria Ternan played opposite him, as Wardour's estranged lover, and experienced the force of Dickens's acting so powerfully that the tears ran down her face in the closing scene. At rehearsals she had complained that 'I cried so much when I saw it, that I have a dread of it, and I don't know what to do'.

But the real depths of emotion were sounded by Dickens himself after the curtain had fallen. Within a few days of their arrival in Manchester, Dickens became obsessed with Ellen Ternan. 'I have never known,' he wrote to Wilkie Collins, 'a moment's peace or contentment, since the last night of *The Frozen Deep*. I do suppose that there never was a man so seized and rended by one spirit.' Ellen Ternan was then eighteen years old, just a year older than his sister-in-law Mary Hogarth had been when she died in his arms so many years before. If the image of Mary had haunted him ever since, then in Ellen Ternan he glimpsed some reawakening of her spirit.

As soon as he conceived this extraordinary passion for the young girl, he felt all the more keenly the constrictions of his own thwarted and unhappy life. He was possessed by what he described as 'grim despair and restlessness'; he simply wanted to 'slink into a corner and cry'. He now confessed to Forster that he found his own wife to be an intolerable burden; they made each other 'uneasy and unhappy', and yet there seemed to be no possibility of separation or divorce. A writer who had celebrated domestic harmony and familial affection could hardly drag his wife through the courts. He was trapped as surely as any of

Above: Ellen Ternan.

the characters in his fictions. In the novel he was composing, *Little Dorrit*, the whole world appears as a gigantic prison and all its inhabitants prisoners.

> *The room looked down into the darkening prison-yard, with its inmates strolling here and there, leaning out of windows, communing as much apart as they could with friends who were going away, and generally wearing out their imprisonment as they best might, that summer evening. The air was heavy and hot; the closeness of the place, oppressive; and from without there arose a rush of free sounds, like the jarring memory of such things in a headache and heartache. She stood at the window, bewildered, looking down into this prison as if it were out of her own different prison...*
>
> Little Dorrit, *Book the Second, Chapter XXXI*

He conceived means of escape from his own life. The success of *The Frozen Deep* reawakened earlier plans for a series of public readings from his books. But for the moment the scheme was laid aside in preparation for another novel; in the atmosphere of his house, however, no such extended work could be written. When Ellen Ternan and her family began an acting tour in the north of England, he followed her. With Wilkie Collins as a travelling companion he journeyed to Carlisle, Doncaster and Lancaster. He was so perplexed and obsessed that he roamed across the mountains and fells of Cumberland, often in a sea of fog. Collins sensed the character of his companion very well. 'Where another fellow would fall into a footbath of action or emotion, you fall into a mine. Where another fellow would be a painted butterfly, you are a fiery dragon.... A man who can do nothing by halves appears to me to be a fearful man.'

On his return to Tavistock House, he was as miserable and unsettled as ever. He started to lie about his wife's incapacities. He told Miss Burdett Coutts that she had never cared for her children and that the children 'do not – and they never did – care for her'. The daughters, in particular, 'harden into stone figures of girls when they can be got to go near her'. All this was patently and flagrantly untrue. It had been at Dickens's insistence, for example, that she had travelled with him to the United States in 1842, even as she wept at the prospect of separation from her family.

To call Dickens a liar, however, is at best a half-truth. As soon as he conceived an impression, or an opinion, it became a truth. His vision of the world was so powerful that it occluded any commonplace realities. As soon as he believed that his wife did not care for the children, then it was heralded to the world as an unalterable fact; he wished it to be true, and so it became true. The scene of the daughters turning to stone in the presence of their mother might have come out of one of his fictions. And that is the essential truth of the matter: he saw the world in terms of Dickensian narrative.

Another scene might also have been taken from one of his novels. He gave orders to his domestic servants that the marital bedroom was to be cut in half, and that a partition was to be erected between him and his wife; it was an extraordinary decision, but demonstrates the ruthlessness of Dickens's will even in the affairs closest to home. He argued with Catherine's parents, over this or some other matter, and left the house in a fury; to calm his beating mind he then walked all the way to Gad's Hill Place, a distance of some thirty miles, leaving London for Kent late at night. It is yet another token of the desperate intensity of his nature. It is almost as if he were walking back into his childhood.

In this period, too, a note of melancholy intensity enters his public pronouncements. He gave a speech for the Hospital for Sick Children in Great Ormond Street, for example, in which he lamented the fate of an infant child

Above: The impoverished streets of London featured strongly in Dickens's fiction and public speeches.

lying in an Edinburgh slum with his 'little wasted face, and his little hot, worn hands folded over his breast, and his little bright attentive eyes'. He moved his audience to tears on this occasion but, if Dickens had tears to shed, they were really only for himself.

At some point Catherine Dickens discovered a bracelet that Dickens had purchased for Ellen Ternan; it seems that, by a curious accident, it was sent to her. She was of a somewhat jealous or suspicious nature, and the unexpected arrival of the gift threw her into a passion of sorrowful complaint. She must have implied that Ellen Ternan was already her husband's mistress, and the aspersion must have infuriated Dickens. Only this can account for his anger and his sense of injury both to himself and to Ellen Ternan. He demanded that Catherine visit her and thus assert in the face of the world that there was no compromising situation between the novelist and the much younger woman; Catherine evidently refused. She left the house and returned to her parents. It was almost the final act of a domestic tragedy.

Georgina Hogarth had elected to stay at Tavistock House; in the absence of Catherine, she became guardian of the house and household alike. It could not have been an easy decision for her, effectively to supplant her sister and to alienate her family, but she seems to have had a genuine if innocent love for Dickens. She could not for a moment imagine being exiled from his bright presence, or returning to the dull life of the Hogarths.

For the sake of propriety, however, Dickens decamped to the office of *Household Words* in Wellington Street, where he set up a temporary refuge. The question of propriety was indeed an important one. He was the novelist of family life, after all, in whose books the virtues of domestic happiness had been endlessly celebrated. How might it seem to his readers and to the larger public if he abrogated all the conventional pieties of familial conduct?

He negotiated quietly with the Hogarth family on the terms for a separation – divorce, in the mid-nineteenth century, was out of the question – and Catherine eventually agreed to accept a house and an annual income of £600.

Above: Catherine Dickens in middle age.

The affair might have been amicably settled, except that Dickens discovered that the Hogarths had begun to spread rumours about his relationship with Ellen Ternan – or, it has been surmised, with Georgina Hogarth herself. It was insupportable, almost incredible, that he should be accused of what, in the opinion of contemporary society, amounted to incest by Georgina's own family. 'My father was like a madman,' his daughter admitted at a later date. '…Nothing could surpass the misery and unhappiness of our home.'

His behaviour was indeed extreme. He believed himself to be surrounded by gossip and innuendo, ruinous both to his character and to his career, and he knew also that he was losing control over events. The loss of mastery was the one thing he most feared; it would be tantamount to losing himself. So he decided to issue a public statement in *Household Words*, and in any newspaper that would care to publish it. He denounced 'misrepresentations, most grossly false, most monstrous and most cruel' and 'lately whispered rumours…abominably false'. The notice was headlined 'PERSONAL', but no more open statement could have been made; the vast majority of Dickens's readers knew nothing whatever about the matter, but now they had indeed been enlightened. It was a spectacular misjudgement on his part, which only served to exacerbate an already difficult situation.

He then compounded the fault by writing a letter to one of his business managers, Arthur Smith, revealing the extent of Catherine's mental weaknesses – 'some peculiarity of her character' had impelled her to consign the care of her children to their aunt Georgina. He authorized Arthur Smith to show the letter to any interested party – and, of course, it too ended up in the columns of the newspapers. It is possible that Dickens did not anticipate its publication. He was in a harassed and dangerous state, in which his decisions were not always wise or considered. It had always been a mark of his character, also, to express in words of fire that which he felt most powerfully.

But the effect was immediate. The newspapers turned upon him, accusing him of hypocrisy and treachery. There were even more serious charges

levelled against him. One newspaper alluded to the rumour of a love affair
with his sister-in-law by stating, 'Let Mr Dickens remember that the odious –
and we might almost add unnatural – profligacy of which he has been accused
would brand him with lifelong infamy.' This year, 1858, was also the summer
of what became known as 'the great stink', when all the effluent discharged
into the Thames began to reek. Lime was poured into the river, and sheets
soaked with chlorine put against the windows of Parliament. The chaos of
the inner world and the outer world were coming together in a great miasma.
He raged against anyone whom he believed to have taken Catherine's part.
He shunned any contact with the printers of *Household Words*, Bradbury and
Evans, because they had refused to insert his 'personal' statement in their
publication *Punch*. He quarrelled with Thackeray, and the already somewhat
difficult relationship between them was severed. It is evidence of Dickens's
hard and somewhat imperious nature.

Above: The Great Stink of the Thames, 1858.

CHAPTER NINE

Public and private

But what of the relationship between Dickens and his readers? Had the accounts of his marital troubles materially influenced their judgement upon him or upon his works? He decided that the matter must be put to the test. He had already conducted public readings of his works in London but, acting against the advice of his closest friends, he prepared to embark upon a grand national tour. 'I must do *something*,' he wrote to Forster, 'or I shall wear my heart away.' He selected various readings from *A Christmas Carol* and other of the Christmas books, and created comic episodes out of *The Pickwick Papers* and *Martin Chuzzlewit*. A new phase of his career began out of impulse and fearfulness.

He need not have been concerned, however, with the public response. His first appearance was greeted with prolonged applause and cheering, and the enthusiasm did not abate during the entire course of the tour. It was his habit to stride across the stage, precisely on time, with a colourful flower in his buttonhole. He never seemed to notice the enthusiasm that greeted his arrival, but waited quite calmly until the applause had subsided. He stood before a maroon screen, with a small reading table and carafe of water in front of him. He pretended to read from a book but, in truth, he had his stories by heart.

Above: Charles Dickens giving a public reading.
Opposite: Dickens dreams about his characters.

And then, when he began, he was transformed. He became each of his characters in turn, so that it seemed to some that he performed some act of magic or alchemy. He adopted all the gestures and expressions of Sam Weller or Mrs Gamp, of Scrooge or Tiny Tim, so that these fictive creatures seemed literally to be alive upon the stage. The audiences laughed so much that Dickens himself could not refrain from laughing with them; in the more poignant passages, large numbers of men and women broke down and wept. It has been suggested that in some way he mesmerized these audiences, but the miracle of his creative gifts does not need so banal an explanation.

Dickens finished a six-week season in London before travelling to Liverpool, Worcester, Exeter and a host of other provincial towns and cities; he travelled to Ireland, where the welcome in Belfast and Cork and Dublin was no less tumultuous. People queued all night for tickets, and lines of policemen were engaged to restrain the waiting crowds. It was a matter of great satisfaction to him that he had in a sense 'faced down' his critics, and he had the additional pleasure of earning a great deal of money from the experience.

Nothing could remove or alleviate, however, the sorrowful mysteries he had so recently endured. 'Sometimes,' he wrote, 'I cannot bear it. I had one of these fits yesterday, and was utterly desolate and lost.' He had placed Ellen Ternan and her sister, Maria, in lodgings off Oxford Street, having taken the precaution of dispatching her mother and elder sister, Fanny, to Italy. It was a measure of his anger or resentment that he was still ill disposed towards those whom he believed to have crossed him. He decided peremptorily to finish his association with Bradbury and Evans by closing down *Household Words*. He planned a new periodical, *All the Year Round*, under his exclusive proprietorship. The printers tried to prevent him by legal means, but their efforts proved to be of no avail. It would seem that nobody but a fool or madman would attempt to cross Charles Dickens. The new periodical duly appeared with a series by its eminent 'conductor' on the title page; almost at once the circulation of the new magazine trebled that of its immediate predecessor.

CHARLES [John Huffman] DICKENS'
The great Novelist appears in various characters, all, however, showing the same prolific "head" — Dickens, alias Pickwick, alias Copperfield, alias Sam Weller, &c, &c.

The new story was entitled *A Tale of Two Cities*; originally he had considered calling it 'Buried Alive', which may reflect something of his state of mind at the time of composition. It is set during the French Revolution, and yet it is in large part a tale of Sydney Carton's hopeless and thwarted passion for a young woman. It seems that Dickens had first conceived the story while dying upon the stage in *The Frozen Deep*, in the company of Ellen Ternan, and the narrative bears all the marks of that turbulent period.

Above: Charles Dickens playing all the parts of his characters.

Waste forces within him, and a desert all around, this man stood still on his way across a silent terrace, and saw for a moment, lying in the wilderness before him, a mirage of honourable ambition, self-denial and perseverance. In the fair city of this vision there were airy galleries from which the loves and graces looked upon him, gardens in which the fruit of life hung ripening, waters of Hope that sparkled in his sight. A moment, and it was gone. Climbing to a high chamber in a well of houses, he threw himself down in his clothes on a neglected bed, and its pillow was wet with wasted tears. Sadly, sadly, the sun rose; it rose upon no sadder sight than the man of good abilities and good emotions, incapable of their directed exercise, incapable of his own help and his own happiness, sensible of the blight on him, and resigning himself to let it eat him away.

A Tale of Two Cities, *Chapter V*

Yet, in a sense, he had triumphed over the events of the recent past. The artist W.P. Frith painted his portrait during this period; it shows the novelist with an eager and determined expression, sitting easily in his chair in a settled position of authority. Frith himself believed that he had depicted a man 'who had reached the topmost rung of a very high ladder and was perfectly aware of his position'. A measure of that awareness can be found in a remark to Frith himself, when the artist could not forbear commenting on Dickens's public readings. 'Whenever I am wrong,' Dickens told him, 'I am obliged to anyone who will tell me of it; but up to the present I have never been wrong.' It was said in jest, but it contains more than a tincture of serious self-admiration.

If he had ever looked objectively at the life of his immediate family, however, that admiration might have waned a little. Catherine was banished to perpetual exile in Camden Town; the eldest son, Charles, lived with her as unofficial guardian, while Kate Dickens frequently visited the house in

Above: Title page of A Tale of Two Cities.

Gloucester Crescent. Kate had felt guilty about her father's treatment of her mother, and was unhappy about Georgina's presence in the household; the visits to her mother were her act of defiance against a father whose weaknesses she perceived very well.

She seems to have been so eager to leave the family, in fact, that she decided upon marriage to a very unsuitable suitor; in a somewhat tense ceremony she married Charles Collins, Wilkie Collins's brother, who was in a state of constant ill health and was rumoured to be homosexual. Dickens did not approve the marriage at all and, on the night of his daughter's departure for her honeymoon, he was found sobbing in her bedroom clutching her bridal dress. 'But for me,' he told his other daughter, Mary, 'Katie would not have left home.'

His own brothers were a perplexing problem. One died, considerately leaving a widow and five children on Dickens's hands, while the others were engaged in protracted periods of cadging from him or complaining about him. His mother still survived into a weak old age and insisted upon dressing up, in Dickens's words, 'in sables, like a female Hamlet'. When he visited her, in a house he had rented for her on Haverstock Hill, 'the instant she saw me, she plucked up a spirit, and asked me for "a pound"'.

His sons, too, were proving a burden to him. They seemed to have inherited nothing from their father except a propensity for restlessness. He could not bequeath them his energy or his determination, since those qualities had been formed upon the anvil of adversity. He sometimes feared that they more closely resembled John Dickens than their immediate parent. It is as if he were some freak of nature. He had no predecessors, and

Above: Dickens with his daughters Mamey and Katey at Gad's Hill Place.
Opposite: William Powell Frith's portrait of Dickens, 1859.

seemed doomed to be without successors. Georgina Hogarth was also very ill with an unspecified ailment of the heart; he had come to rely upon his sister-in-law for maintaining a semblance of domesticity in his life in the surroundings of Gad's Hill, and he could scarcely imagine life without her.

He had decided to sell Tavistock House and to convert Gad's Hill Place into his permanent residence. His decision was based upon an apparent disinclination to live in London, but in truth the memories of the house were still too strong for his composure. From this time forward he merely rented houses for the London 'season'. He repudiated the past in another fashion, too, by making a bonfire of all his letters in the garden behind Gad's Hill. All the correspondence from his contemporaries – from Tennyson, from Carlyle, from George Eliot, from Thackeray – was consigned to the flames in a grand gesture of rejection.

It is significant, perhaps, that in a series of essays for *All the Year Round* he took on the role of a wanderer or 'Uncommercial Traveller'; in these short pieces he rediscovers the terrors and delights of childhood, as well as all the mysteries of London. He describes his night walks through the city, and his journeys to City graveyards; he depicts the vagrant and the outcast as if he possessed a fellow feeling for them; he describes the prisons and asylums. All the restlessness and unhappiness of his life fill his disquisitions on the nature of loneliness and on the nature of confinement.

In the pages of *All the Year Round*, too, he had begun a new weekly serial which bore all the marks of his private preoccupations. It was entitled *Great Expectations*, and was recognized almost at once as one of the finest of his novels. The narrative was set in the area of Rochester and the Medway, which now of course he had made his permanent home, and the vicissitudes of Dickens's own childhood can be discovered darkly and obliquely in the diminutive figure of Pip. He is the blacksmith's boy who unexpectedly finds a rich anonymous patron to guide him

Top: Kate, Mamey and Charles Dickens with H.F.Chorley, Charles A. Collins and Georgina Hogarth on the front steps of Gad's Hill.
Above: Henry Fielding Dickens.

through the world; by describing his
ingratitude towards his childhood
companion, the blacksmith Joe Gargery,
he seems in some part to be coming to terms
with his own past as the boy in the blacking
factory. But there are other elements at
work. As in its predecessor, *A Tale of Two Cities*,
the narrative is in part devoted to the cause
of hopeless and helpless love.

I knew to my sorrow, often and often, if not always, that I loved her against reason, against promise, against peace, against hope, against happiness, against all discouragement that could be. Great Expectations, *Chapter XXIX*

In the figures of Lucie Manette in *A Tale of Two Cities* and Estella in *Great Expectations* he is creating a twin image of the unobtainable young woman who haunts the passionate consciousness of an unsuccessful lover. Whether this has any echo in Dickens's own heart, or bears any relation to his intimacy with Ellen Ternan, cannot now be known. But it is a suggestive and provoking coincidence none the less. And can Estella's words have a resonance elsewhere in Dickens's life? 'I have no heart. Oh, I have a heart to be stabbed in or shot in, I have no doubt, and, of course, if it ceased to beat I should cease to be. But you know what I mean. I have no softness there, no sympathy – sentiment – nonsense.' It throws a tentative light, if nothing else, upon the mysteries of an intimate friendship which seem to have caused him nothing but anxiety and despair.

In his correspondence with his closest friends he merely hints at his private 'troubles', but there can be little doubt that his intimacy provoked unhappiness as much as it provided comfort. He had moved Ellen and her family to a house off the Hampstead Road, and it seems likely that she stayed at Gad's Hill Place on a number of occasions. There are later reports that they

Above: Dickens's study at Gad's Hill Place.

sang together in the evenings, but very little else is known about their intimacy. There have been rumours of illegitimate children, of a child that died. But no evidence has emerged to warrant such speculation.

At a later date he established Ellen and her mother in a cottage near Boulogne and often visited them there. He also rented them accommodation in Peckham, and stayed in the vicinity under the name of 'Mr Tringham'.

His daughter Kate once wrote that their relationship was 'more tragic and far-reaching in its effect…than that of Nelson and Lady Hamilton'; the remark does not imply any joyful union. Ellen Ternan is supposed to have declared that 'she loathed the very thought of the intimacy'. But if this suggests an unhappy or unwilling liaison, it is at least clear from other reports that she maintained it until the very end of Dickens's life. The rest is rumour.

The original conclusion of *Great Expectations* had depicted the disillusion of Pip, and a melancholy recognition of the failure of his love for Estella. But Bulwer Lytton objected to the pathos of this ending, and argued that the young companions should be reunited in the final scenes. He believed that the public would otherwise feel disappointed or dissatisfied. Dickens saw the force of his objections, and changed the novel in proof form.

He respected his public too much to risk any offence. He needed that public, also, as a bulwark against his own encroaching disappointments and sorrows.

It is significant that in *A Tale of Two Cities* and *Great Expectations* the image of the prison once more emerges. Dr Manette had been imprisoned in the Bastille for eighteen years and must in some sense be restored to life; the fate of Pip in *Great Expectations* is determined by the ex-convict, and inhabitant of the prison 'hulks', Magwitch. In the same period Dickens might have been forgiven for thinking that he too lived in the shadow of the prison house.

Above: Playing cards at Miss Havisham's in Great Expectations.

His contemporaries were dying around him, and he wrote to Forster that
'…all ways have the same finger post at the head of them, and at every
turning in them'. He still firmly believed that life represented a battle
that must be fought to the end – 'Never SAY die' was his motto in all
circumstances – but there were times of distress when his resolution faltered.

If he had grown weary or disillusioned, he laboured to subdue his own
feelings in a round of activity. He decided to embark
upon a new series of readings, and travelled to Paris in
order to read at the British Embassy there. He was so
restless that he considered proposals for an Australian
tour. His financial commitments were now in fact so
extensive that, rich as he was, he seemed determined to
make as much money as possible; but the prospect of six
months away, in particular away from Ellen Ternan,
proved unendurable to him. The Australian plans
were postponed.

Instead he began work upon what would be his last
completed novel, *Our Mutual Friend*. He rented a house
near Hyde Park for the early months of 1865; to be in
London, however much he now disliked it, was to be at
the very heart of his inspiration. But his old faculty of
energetic composition had in part deserted him; he was
progressing slowly and showed the first signs of

manifest ill-health. His left foot was badly swollen and continually painful.
He ascribed this affliction variously to gout and to frostbite, but in fact he was
showing the first symptoms of the arterial disease that would eventually kill
him. He was not one who succumbed easily to physical disorders of any kind,
however, and despite the fact that he sometimes professed himself 'lame',
he continued with his daily walks of ten miles or more. It is a measure of
his stamina no less than of the power of his will.

Above: Kate Dickens.

CHAPTER TEN

Last years

On 9 June 1865, Dickens returned from France in the company of Ellen Ternan and her mother. They boarded the 2.38 'tidal train' at Folkestone for their journey back to London; thirty-three minutes later they passed the

Above: The Railway Station by William Powell Frith, 1863.

town of Headcorn and, at a speed of fifty miles per hour, were approaching the viaduct over the River Beult just outside Staplehurst. Repair work was being conducted on the line, but the foreman had consulted the wrong timetable and did not expect the onrushing train. The tracks had been taken up and there was a gap of forty feet. The train arched and fell into the riverbed below.

Dickens and the Ternans were trapped in a swaying carriage, just above the wreckage. Ellen cried out in horror, but he caught hold of her. 'We can't help

ourselves,' he said, 'but we can be quiet and composed. Pray don't cry out.'
He clambered out of the carriage and approached two train guards who were
running in confusion.

'Pray, stop a second,' he said, 'Do you know me?'

'We know you very well, Mr Dickens.'

They surrendered their keys to him. He helped the Ternans out of
their carriage and then began his work among the dead and the dying lying
alongside the riverbed. He filled his top hat with water and, with the additional
aid of a brandy flask, tried to give some comfort to the injured.

And then he did a remarkable thing. He remembered that he had left
that month's manuscript of *Our Mutual Friend* in the swaying carriage. So in
the calmest possible way he clambered back into the compartment and
rescued it. But he was not calm for very long. He felt the effects of nausea for
days afterwards; his pulse was unsteady, and he experienced all the physical
tremors of nervous anxiety. He declared that he felt 'quite shattered and
broken up'. Indeed, the accident haunted him for the rest of his life. He was
filled with nervous fear on later journeys, even in hansom cabs, and his son
said that he never fully recovered from the shock. It cannot be coincidence,
also, that he died on the same date, 9 June, only five years later.

By rescuing the instalment of *Our Mutual Friend* from the railway carriage,
he helped to preserve for posterity one of the
darkest of his novels. In it, the whole of English
society is compared to a gigantic dust-heap in
which money, and the pursuit of money, are
the only imperatives. All the appurtenances of
'society' are designed only to camouflage greed
and desire. There were also mournful touches
of another kind.

One of Dickens's characters is brought back
to life but 'like us all, every day of our lives when

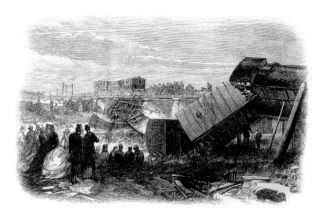

Above: Staplehurst train crash, 5 June 1865.
Opposite: Charles Dickens helping the injured of the Staplehurst crash.

we wake – he is instinctively unwilling to be restored to consciousness, and would be left dormant if he could'. There seems to be a trace of fellow feeling here, confirming, if nothing else, that Dickens himself had lost the exuberance and energy of his earlier years. In this novel, too, there are all the signs and symptoms of thwarted passion. 'If I were shut up in a strong prison,' Bradley Headstone tells Lizzie Hexam, 'you would draw me out. I should break through the wall to come to you. If I were lying on a sick bed, you would draw me up – to stagger to your feet and fall there.' The lineaments of imaginative sorrow spring here from some intuitive knowledge drawn from Dickens's own self.

It was a foggy day in London, and the fog was heavy and dark...Even in the surrounding country it was a foggy day, but there the fog was grey, whereas in London it was, at about the boundary line, dark yellow, and a little within it brown, and then browner, and then browner, until at the heart of the City — St Mary Axe — it was rusty-black. From any point of the high ridge of land northward, it might have been discerned that the loftiest buildings made an occasional struggle to get their heads above the foggy sea, and especially that the great dome of Saint Paul's seemed to die hard; but this was not perceivable in the streets at their feet, where the whole metropolis was a heap of vapour charged with muffled sound of wheels, and enfolding a gigantic catarrh.

Our Mutual Friend, *Book the Third*

Whatever his private tribulations, however, Dickens had lost none of his reforming zeal. In this last completed novel he rails against all the evils of a pernicious 'system', with its gaols and its workhouses, its mechanical sympathies and its mercenary provisions. It is a world of exploitation and cruelty, and in a postscript to the novel Dickens adverts to 'the shameful cases of disease and death from destitution'. He had lost none of his anger, either, so that the tone and temper of *Our Mutual Friend* have all the disruptive energy of *Oliver Twist* or *Nicholas Nickleby*. To use one of his own favourite metaphors, he was fighting the battle until the very end.

His health was steadily declining in the process. He began to suffer various

pains in his chest and stomach, as well as in his eyes; all these ailments were connected with a degeneration in his heart, and he reported to Georgina Hogarth that 'I have noticed for some time a decided change in my buoyancy and hopefulness – in other words, in my usual "tone"'. But he never once considered any relaxation of his always frantic activity; his instinct, strange though it may seem, was actually to increase the load of business he was forced to bear. It is almost as if he wished to punish himself in some ill-defined way for all the weaknesses of the flesh.

It was in this period, for example, that he arranged another reading tour of the entire country – even though he was obliged to travel by train, the one mode of transport which, after the Staplehurst disaster, he could not endure. With a new business manager, George Dolby, he journeyed up and down England. Dolby himself has left a memoir of his employer, whom he describes in vivid terms. In his account, for example, Dickens's eyes – which had once been compared by another writer to 'danger lamps' – were said to contain 'the iron will of a demon and the tender pity of an angel'. He might have added that they also contained the hilarity of a natural clown. Dolby reports on Dickens's antics during their journeys – how he danced the hornpipe in their first-class carriage, and how he knocked on various household doors in Portsmouth before running away. In the bathroom of one hotel he mimicked the gestures of the clown Joe Grimaldi, and then accidentally fell into the bath. His high

Above: Dickens in his last years.

spirits could not be put down, and in this effusion of hilarity even amid ill-health and sorrow we see a true picture of Dickens in the world.

Even as his health grew worse, he planned new reading tours. He sometimes relapsed into general faintness and sickness, but in an act of self-deception he ascribed these symptoms to the effects of the Staplehurst crash rather than to any physical indisposition. In any case, he was busy again in Liverpool and in Newcastle, in Wolverhampton and in Birmingham. He even managed a tour of Ireland in the middle of Fenian unrest. But then came the most extraordinary decision of all. He would return to America in order to make another fortune.

He had not forgotten his earlier reception, when the press had turned savagely against him; soon afterwards, he had published the anti-American chapters of *Martin Chuzzlewit*. He could not be sure, therefore, what welcome he might receive. His friends also remonstrated with him, on the very good grounds that his health might completely break down under the strain of such a tour. He simply replied, in familiar terms, that he preferred to die in action rather than rust in repose.

But there was one more significant objection. The journey to America would mean an enforced separation from Ellen Ternan. 'I should be wretched beyond expression,' he told Forster. First he wanted her to accompany him, despite the manifold dangers of exposure. He suggested that she travel as the ostensible companion to his daughter Mary, but the scheme was abandoned as impractical. Then he devised a scheme whereby she would travel some days after his arrival, and an elaborate code was established for cables sent by telegraph back to England. 'All well' was to be interpreted as 'you come'; 'safe and well' meant that 'you don't come'. But all such plans and devices came to nothing, for the very good reason that Ellen Ternan's reputation would have been thoroughly ruined if she had been seen in the company of Dickens. The risk was too great to be contemplated. Dickens would be accompanied only by his manager.

Even before he embarked, however, his health was under threat. His foot swelled again and he was effectively lamed. Rumours appeared in the American press about his physical condition, and he felt obliged to issue a public statement denying everything and claiming that he 'never was better in his life'. This was manifestly untrue, but his fictional powers were once more stronger than any uncomfortable reality. A great dinner was held for him before his departure. When he rose to speak, a great tumult of cries and cheers erupted; he faltered and the tears ran down his face. In earlier days he would have greeted the enthusiasm with cool deliberation; now, tired and ill, he could not hide his emotion.

He sailed from Liverpool on the *Cuba*; the journey across the Atlantic was uneventful, except for the fact that Dickens was in constant pain, and after ten days the ship docked in Boston. The streets of the city had been swept in honour of his arrival, and the print-shops were filled with photographs of the eminent novelist. As the *New York Times* put it, 'Even in England, Dickens is less known than here…', a pardonable exaggeration in the face of such a welcome. The lines forming for tickets to his readings had reached a length of half a mile, and he was everywhere surrounded by crowds. There were also, of course, less agreeable signs of interest. Reporters haunted his hotel; waiters would peer through the cracks in restaurant doors to watch him eating. 'These people have not in the least changed during the last five and twenty years,' he said. 'They are doing now exactly what they were doing then.' But in time he put aside this harsh verdict and, by the end of his tour, he professed his delight in observing a progress in American manners and morals.

His readings in the United States worked the same alchemical change upon his audiences as in England. The halls were packed to bursting and, in the glare of the gaslight, Dickens would work through all of the transformation scenes in which he became Scrooge and Bob Cratchit, Samuel Weller and Sergeant Buzfuz. To some it seemed that they had been miraculously transported into the pages of the novels; to others, like Longfellow, it was simply a triumph of acting. Dickens himself recorded how 'one poor young girl in mourning burst into a passion of grief about Tiny Tim, and was taken out'.

Ill health was now Dickens's constant and unwelcome companion. He was often faint to the point of prostration after the performance, and there were occasions when what he called a 'cold' or 'catarrh' rendered him practically voiceless; his left foot was still lame, and had to be swathed in bandages. Yet, despite these manifest weaknesses, he managed to nerve himself for each night's reading. One doctor advised him to stop for a period of recuperation, but he refused. He was now eating very little – a boiled egg in the morning, a piece of quail or chicken in the afternoon, and an egg mixed with sherry in the evening. The enormous heat of the hotels and railway carriages plagued him, too. He had always believed in the efficacy of fresh air as a restorative, and had a habit of throwing all the windows of his room open.

He had decided that he would only visit the towns and cities in the east of the United States, but in the six months of his visit he endured a gruelling schedule of 'one night stands' in myriad different places. In Baltimore and Philadelphia he was mobbed. In New York vast crowds waited to catch a glimpse of him. In Washington the President and his entire Cabinet, as well as

Top: Selling tickets for the New York event.
Above: Reception for Dickens held at Delmonicos, Manhattan.

the judges of the Supreme Court, came to witness the spectacle. President Andrew Johnson booked a row of seats for each of the seven nights of the readings.

The public recognition of his genius, however, did not alleviate his private miseries. The enforced separation from Ellen Ternan left him utterly cast down and bewildered; it is as if half of his life had been forcibly taken from

him. According to Dolby, 'the Chief', as he called him, was 'suffering from the most acute depression'. His 'cold' left him continually streaming with tears, but in truth he had other reasons for weeping.

In a speech that he gave after the final reading in New York, he declared that 'the shadow of one word has impended over me all this evening, and the time has come at last when the shadow must fall.' So he said farewell, and the vast audience rose in an outpouring of cheers and tears. As he left New York harbour, on 22 April, he raised his hat upon a cane and called out 'God bless you, every one!' It was a very Dickensian scene.

He arrived at Liverpool in the first days of May and, by happy coincidence, his doctor informed him that he looked seven years younger. This was Dickens's report, at least, but the truth was very different. He had earned some £20,000 by his American venture, but at the cost of his health and strength: he had been gravely weakened by the hard routine that he had pursued, and would never fully recover from the ordeal. Not that he had any intention of stopping or slowing down. Even while on the outbound boat to America, he had been negotiating another English tour of some one hundred readings. There was no one of suffi-

Opposite: The Washington Monument.

cient authority to prevent him from destroying himself. All his life he had followed the precepts and injunctions of his own will, but now that wilfulness would be his undoing.

The roads around Gad's Hill had been decorated with flags to greet the returning hero. He was eager to pick up the threads of his old life, and went back immediately to work on *All the Year Round*; the editorial manager of that enterprise, W.H. Wills, was so seriously ill that all the business fell upon Dickens himself. When Longfellow and his daughters arrived for a holiday in England, however, Dickens lived up to his reputation for conviviality. In Dickensian fashion he took them around Kent in an antique coach that might have come out of *The Pickwick Papers*.

The opening readings in London brought on all the worst symptoms of his illness. His eyes were dimmer, and he could only read the right-hand side of shop signs. All the while he was being cooked by gaslight, his pulse racing as he entered all the imagined agonies and joys of his characters. But then, as it were, he increased the volume. One afternoon his son Charley was sitting in Gad's Hill Place when he heard a furious argument between a man and a woman; it was conducted 'with all the circumstances of aggravated brutality'. Rushing outside, he discovered his father in the act of rehearsing the murder of Nancy by Sikes from *Oliver Twist*. The whole scene, including the shrieks of Nancy and the savage blows of Sikes, was being enacted with the utmost veracity and ferocity. It was the 'sensation' that Dickens required for his next reading tour.

His friends and family strongly advised against it, but he refused to listen to them, and professed himself puzzled by their insistence. He did not seem at all aware of the danger, but it is likely that the effort of reading the 'murder' did indeed hasten his death. It could be argued that, even as Sikes murdered Nancy, Dickens's characters were killing their creator.

And it did indeed create a sensation. Members of the audience fainted during the reconstruction of the death of the young woman. 'If only one woman cries out when you murder this girl,' a friend told him, 'then there will be a contagion of hysteria all over this place.' And yet he insisted on enacting the murder again and again; it was as if the death of this young girl provided his only relief. He had written the novel thirty years before, but now he was drawn back to it. Yet why was he so passionately attached to the terrible scene of the young woman being butchered by her lover? Could it have been part of his unresolved

feelings for Ellen Ternan? Could it have been an expression of his frustration at the course of his own life, which could only be exorcized by an act of passionate violence?

During the course of the reading tour he was so afflicted by lameness that a local doctor advised him not to perform. For once Dickens did not resist the injunction, but his reaction was characteristic. 'It throws us all back, and will cost me some five hundred pounds.' Then he rallied, but a few weeks later he was overwhelmed by a feeling 'of weakness and deadness...on the left side'. His private physician, Thomas Beard, was summoned. At his instigation, all further readings were cancelled. Dickens had been on the edge of a paralytic stroke.

The following month, in May 1869, Dickens drew up the provisions of his will, in which he left the sum of £1000 to 'Miss Ellen Lawless Ternan'. Surely he must have known that the nature of their liaison would be discussed after his death. He also stipulated that 'those who attend my funeral wear no scarf, cloak, black bow, long hatband, or other such revolting absurdity'. Even after his demise, he would disparage the customs of society.

He must indeed had have had some sense that his death was approaching. There are accounts in this period of how susceptible he had become; how much more ready he was to break down in tears. Yet he continued to labour while it was still light. He supervised the publication of *All the Year Round* and,

with the enforced interruption of his readings, began
seriously to contemplate the composition of a new novel.
It was to be quite unlike anything he had ever written.
The Mystery of Edwin Drood would be precisely that – a 'mystery'
in which the elements of detection are mixed with some of
the most fanciful themes and images of his writing career.
It seems likely that he was taking laudanum, or tincture of
opium, to alleviate the pains of his illness; the novel itself
opens in an opium den in the East End of London, and the
twin themes of crime and guilt rise with the fumes of that
soporific. He had resumed his own wanderings around
London, too. Upon the arrival of some American friends, he
conducted them around the less salubrious areas of the city.
They noticed how he observed every scene of hardship and
of poverty; how he took a ragged infant from the arms of its
ailing mother. It was as if he had re-entered his old kingdom.

*There was music playing here and there, but it did not enliven the case. No
barrel organ mended the matter, and no big drum beat dull care away. Like the
chapel bells that were also going here and there, they only seemed to evoke echoes
from brick surfaces, and dust from everything. As to the flat wind-instruments,
they seemed to have cracked their hearts and souls in pining for the country.*

The Mystery of Edwin Drood, *Chapter XX*

In the last year of his life Dickens continued work on the new novel. In the
contract for its publication, there had been a clause, that stated a financial
compromise would be reached by his heirs and publishers in the event of his
death; he was not convinced, in other words, that he would ever finish it.
He had rented a house near Hyde Park for the early months of the year.

Opposite: A destitute boy on the streets.
Above: Police searching the streets of Victorian England.

He seemed in relatively good spirits, too, despite the fact that the left side of his body provoked in him curious uneasiness and pain. He was also anticipating with pleasure a short series of public readings in London; the prospect of performing and acting before an audience allowed him a curious escape from the more sombre realities of life. But he had not abandoned his public involvement in the affairs of the day, or indeed in the spirit of the century. He attended a prize-giving at the Birmingham and Midland Institute, where he announced that 'My faith in the people governing is, on the whole, infinitesimal; my faith in The People governed is, on the whole, illimitable.' It may not seem a very profound statement but, after a lifetime of controversy and argument, the simplest words are often the truest.

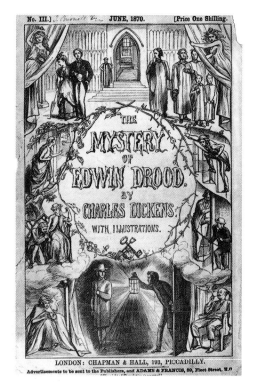

Dickens's latest and last set of public readings proved to be his undoing. He could not pronounce the name of 'Pickwick', as if some function of his brain or memory had been impaired. In the intervals between the readings he retired to his dressing room badly lamed and quite unable to speak; he lay down for ten minutes, voiceless and nerveless, until he had sufficiently recovered to mount the platform once again. His doctor had ordered some steps to be put beside that platform and told Charley that 'you must be there every night, and, if you see your father falter in the least, you must run and catch him and bring him off to me, or by Heaven, he'll die before them all'.

Yet, of course, Dickens managed to conclude the series, as he knew he must, without once disappointing his large and attentive audiences. He made a speech upon the last night, as he stood crying in the gaslight, infinitely sad and wearied by a lifetime of performances but still not broken. 'From these garish lights,' he announced, 'I now vanish for ever more, with a heartfelt, grateful, respectful, affectionate farewell.' It was followed by a storm of cheering.

Above: Frontispiece of The Mystery of Edwin Drood.

The Queen invited him for an audience, and such was her respect for the prematurely ageing and infirm novelist, that she stood for the entire length of the interview. It was rumoured that she had offered him a peerage, or a seat on her Privy Council, but Dickens always insisted that he would remain simply 'Charles Dickens'. It was the name upon his novels and would far outlive any public honour.

To all observers his outward behaviour was still that of an active man of the world. *The Mystery of Edwin Drood* was selling more than any of its immediate predecessors, and was hailed even by the critics as a return to the novelist's 'old' jovial manner. In the last full month of his life, too, he was still engaged in the 'old' habits of his early youth. He had decided, for example, to become stage manager and director for some private theatricals at the house of a friend.

A few days before his death he was writing *The Mystery of Edwin Drood* in the office of *All the Year Round*. Charley knocked upon the door, and entered. 'After a moment I said, "If you don't want anything more, sir, I shall be off now," but he continued his writing with the same intensity as before, and gave no sign of being aware of my presence. Again I spoke – louder, perhaps this time – and he raised his head and looked at me long and fixedly. But I soon found that, although his eyes were bent upon me, and he

Above: Interior at Gad's Hill Place and the desk on which Dickens wrote his last letter.

seemed to be looking at me earnestly, he did not see me, and that he was in fact unconscious of my existence. He was in dreamland with Edwin Drood, and I left him – for the last time.' In some of the later passages of that novel he was depicting in sorrowful terms the 'river winding down from the mist on the horizon, as though that were its source, and already heaving with a restless knowledge of its approach to the sea'.

He left London for the last time at the beginning of June 1870, and returned to Gad's Hill Place. For the next two or three days he maintained his regular routine of writing and walking; he arranged for a few small 'improvements' in the house, and spent the evenings in the company of Georgina and his daughters. On Wednesday, 8 June, against his practice, he spent much of the day writing the novel in a chalet that had been erected for him in the spacious garden. He came back to the house in the evening, where he wrote two or three letters.

At dinner that night, Georgina noticed that he looked unwell. He replied that he had been very ill for some hours. When she asked for a doctor to be called, he said something about returning to London. He rose from his chair but, under the influence of some fit or stroke, he fell; she held him in her arms, but then laid him quietly on the floor. A doctor was summoned from Rochester, and Dickens was carried to a sofa in the dining room. He never stirred from it again. His daughters had already returned to London, but a telegram brought them back at once. Ellen Ternan, too, arrived at Gad's Hill. Charley was dispatched to inform his mother. Dickens lay dying, breathing slowly and loudly through that night and the next day. Then, at six on the following evening, Thursday, 9 June 1870, a tear rolled down his cheek and he died.

Thomas Carlyle called his death 'an event world-wide', and Longfellow wrote from America that 'It is no exaggeration to say that this whole country is stricken with grief.' Immediately after the news of his death was announced, The Times suggested that Dickens should be buried in Westminster Abbey, the

Opposite: Dickens's writing chalet in the grounds of Gad's Hill Place.

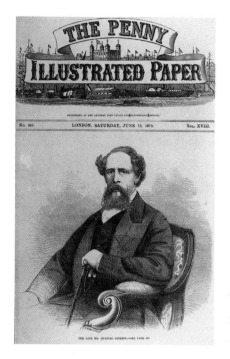

final home for so many of England's most eminent writers. He had asked to be interred quietly in Rochester Cathedral, but the will and wish of the nation had to be respected. It would remain a private ceremony, however, according to the provisions of his last testament.

The body was brought up from Gad's Hill to Charing Cross in a special train and, in the company of his immediate family, he was interred beneath the flagstones of the abbey. Neither Catherine Dickens nor Ellen Ternan was present at the burial. Yet the people of England came, in their thousands, to pay their own respects to the writer who more than any other seemed to understand their lives. He represented, and celebrated, their world in all its humour and its pathos, its energy and its violence, its exuberance and its sorrow. He was, in the strictest sense, the Inimitable.

Top: Death of Dickens given in The Penny.
Above: Memorial in Westminster Abbey.
Opposite: Dickens on his deathbed by John Everett Millais.

INDEX

Page numbers in *italic* refer to illustrations

PICTURE CREDITS

AKG p16, p42, pp69–70, p72, p75, p79, p80; **Barnardo's** p97, p150; **BBC/Jane Mayes** p27 bottom; **Dickens House Museum** p6 middle, p6 bottom, p8, p10, p14 bottom, p17, p24, p26 right, p27 top, p29 bottom, p30, p32 bottom, p.40 top and bottom, pp46–8, pp62–3, p65, p71, p74, p78, p82, p84, p89, p93, p98, p103, p113 top and bottom, p119 top, pp131–3, p136 bottom, p.139, pp143–4, p147 top and bottom, p156 top and bottom, p157; **Dickens House Museum, London/Bridgeman Art Library** p15; **Guildhall Library, Corporation of London, UK/ Bridgeman Art Library** pp12–13, p37, p45, p101 top; **Hammersmith and Fulham Archives and Local History Centre** p88; **Hulton Archive** p6 top, p11, p13 top, p14 top, pp20–1, p26 left, p29 top, p31, pp33–4, p35 bottom, p38, p43, p49, p51 bottom, pp52–3, p56 bottom, p57, p59 top, pp67–8, p81 top, p101 bottom, p104, p106, p108, p109 bottom, p114, p118, pp122–4, p126–7, p130, p134, p136 top, p138, pp152–4; **Library of Congress, Washington D.C., USA/Bridgeman Art Library** p55; **Mansell/Timepix/Rex Features** p96; **Mary Evans Picture Library** p7, pp18–19, pp22–3, p28, p32 top, p39, p41, p51 top, p56 top, p58, p59 bottom, pp60–1, p64, p77, p81 bottom, p83, pp85–7, p90, p92, pp94–5, p99, pp111–12, pp116–17, p119 bottom, p121, p129, p137, p142, p148, p151; **Museum of London** p9; **National Maritime Museum** p54; **National Portrait Gallery** p109 top; **New Walk Museum, Leicester City Museum Service, UK/Bridgeman Art Library** pp140–1; **Private Collection/Bridgeman Art Library** p36, p102; **V&A Picture Library** p35 top; **Victoria and Albert Museum/Bridgeman Art Library** p135.